To Peter an
Happy men
halcyon days in zam...

Zambia Stole My Heart

affectionately your
thorpin

C000048666

Zambia Stole My Heart

Volume One
of the memoirs of

Merfyn Temple

Edited by
Ruth Quine
and
Roland Lubett

With line drawings by
Tania Lubett
from the author's photographs

millipede books

Published by
Millipede Books,
41a Portnall Road,
London W9 3BA

Copyright © Merfyn Temple, 2010

ISBN-10: 0-9530369-1-X
ISBN-13: 978-0-9530369-1-2
EAN: 9780953036912

The text of Chapters 12 to 19 of this book was previously published in *Elephants and Millipedes* (Millipede Books, 1997)

The editors also gratefully acknowledge permission from the following to reproduce extracts of copyright material:

The Methodist Church for 'Kindled in Some Hearts it is', from *The Widening Way: Northern Rhodesian Sketches,* ed. E.G. Nightingale, Cargate Press, 1952
The Methodist Recorder, for the article 'Federation' from *Young Britain,* 1953
The British Library's Sound Archive, Methodist Sound Archive, for the prayer tape on Zambian Independence, October 1964

Every effort has been made to obtain permission for other copyright works. The publishers regret any omissions and would be pleased to hear from any copyright owners where permission has not been granted or acknowledgement not made.

Set in Dante MT Standard
Printed by Lightning Source

Contents

Foreword   viii

From the Editors   xi

Preface   xii

Prologue   1

1   Planted in Methodist Soil   3

2   Wrestling with School   15

3   First Steps into Africa   29

4   Nambala: Settling In   39

5   Nambala: Home and Family   47

6   Nambala: Evangelism and Ministry   60

7   Nambala: Preaching Farmers   74

8   Winds of Change   88

9   Town and Politics   98

10   Working for Kaunda   112

11   Chipapa   123

12   Shachifwa's Story   127

13   Village Life   136

14   Chipapa Diary 1   144

15   Chipapa Diary 2   155

16   Water Tales   166

17   The Chiloto Bus   179

18   A Parliament of Birds   190

19   Time to Leave   197

Epilogue: Return to the First World   209

Photographs

The four Temple boys   5

Ruth Barrowclough, Merfyn's mother   7

John Temple, Merfyn's father   10

The boys and their father at the beach   12

Merfyn at the Leys School   21

Newly ordained   27

Arrival in Cape Town   30

The wedding at Chipembi, 1946   43

The Temples' house at Nambala mission   47

Merfyn and Audrey carry baby Ruth   49

Mary Jane, Audrey, and Ruth, 1949   54

Merfyn farewells the family as he sets off on his bicycle   57

Team of porters   62

Preaching at Mono village   67

Audrey with the Sisterhood, local women's fellowship   70

Village boys play with kittens as their mother cooks   77

Laughing boys atop a bountiful maize harvest   82

Colin Morris, Merfyn and Kaunda at work on *Black Government?* (*Northern News*)   105

The children on a break near Livingstone   109

The family outside their Lusaka house   126

Merfyn fasts for world poverty (*Daily Telegraph*)   137

A proud Merfyn welcomes President Kaunda on a visit to Chipapa   139

Another fast, over the state of the Chipapa road (*Lusaka Times*)   142

Chipapa vehicle 1: the Ford Popular   147

Sarah Kalambalala   149

Off to work in Chipapa's gardens   151

Merfyn at his Chipapa house   157

Chipapa vehicle 2: the vanette   162

A Chipapa tomato grower offers her produce for sale   169

The well at Chipapa   171

Chipapa's key resource: the dam   174

Chipapa vehicle 3: the Chiloto bus   185

Getting the tomato harvest ready for market   187

Flocks of ducks and geese on the dam   194

Discussion group   200

"Fighting Parson Bows Out" (*Lusaka Times*)   202

Merfyn in relaxed mood in Chipapa   205

Maps

Central Zambia   28

Chipapa and surrounding area   122

Chipapa village   145

Foreword

Merfyn Temple's memoirs take us through a personal journey of inner struggle and conquest. As a child and through school and college, Merfyn faced challenges that he always managed to bring under control to his ultimate advantage. This is the journey of a young man of twenty-one years who comes to a foreign country armed only with the armour of the Good News and his strong family background of service.

After some months in Broken Hill and Kafue he went to Nambala, his designated station, over 100 miles west of Lusaka. The challenge to the people was how to meet simple basic needs such as water, food, health. The heroine of health was his medical doctor wife, Audrey Gray; but Merfyn worked with her to inform his flock about the available medical facility and the importance of accessing it. By the Nambala standards of the time, the Temple family lived in a world of material comfort, but theirs was an open house, where many people, including children, came in and out, sometimes spending a night there. To the people of the Nambala area, he became tenderly referred to as *Muluti* (reverend) *Tempulu* because of what he did to the communities, but also because of how the family lived and related to the people.

Muluti Tempulu worked within the Methodist outreach system, to equip the people with tools to live as Christians. But at the same time, he struggled with provision of skills and resources for sustainable livelihoods. To him, denying people the means to secure livelihood was equal to inflicting injustice. The poverty surrounding him at Nambala and which he witnessed during his many travels to the villages made him realize the need to marry speaking to the people with words with speaking to them with hands and actions.

Merfyn and his family confronted material injustice among the people in the Nambala area and in other circuits. However, it was not until his relocation to Kitwe and Lusaka that this growing sense of injustice was articulated. He witnessed it at many levels of his life: in his work life on the Copperbelt and as he journeyed through the country side sometimes with his black colleagues. I remember, as a fresh graduate from rural Chipembi Girls Secondary School, being filled with awe when I went to the Temple home for lunch. It was my first time to visit the white residential area and a white home, apart from the Nambala house, which did not come anywhere near the "muzungu" home in urban areas. But Merfyn was clearly uncomfortable living in this style.

He did not desire to give up church ministry, but he saw politics, the greatest promoter of injustice at the time, as the more effective means to right this injustice. It did not surprise those who knew him that he decided to openly declare his membership in the United National Independence Party, nor when he joined government on a full-time basis. He saw these as platforms from where to fight for justice, and to equip the poor for self-driven fight against their poverty. Given his interest in people's involvement in their own development and in the power or youth and organization, he welcomed his appointment to serve as a leader in the National Service. This would offer him an opportunity both to mobilize the young and to help equip them with the tools he believed could help them meet their livelihoods on a sustainable basis, on the land.

Another opportunity opened up when his family had to move to the United Kingdom for educational reasons. *A la* Temple, he was once again faced with some inner struggle. Was it right that he should remain in his big house in Lusaka? Was it right for him to preach against poverty and injustice when he did not fully understand it, by living it to the greatest extent possible? His years of residence at Chipapa village in very basic conditions summed up both his dream of fighting for social and economic injustice, and his desire to live with the poor and thus understand and help them better. He experienced first-hand problems that people who live in those conditions face every day; how they manage their lives; what their responses are to opportunities and hurdles that may come their way; and the potential in many men and women that remain unexploited.

Researching into rural underdevelopment for my PhD degree, I visited Muluti Tempulu at Chipapa to see how his vision of a socially and economically just world was being played out *in situ*. I was puzzled by the Temple I was reading and hearing about and his efforts among the people he lived with. In my mind, he still was the Tempulu of my childhood Nambala. Sure, I now saw in him a human being living a Biblical Utopia among the poor and thus quite serene at that level. Yet there was some intensity in him I did not remember from when I was five or six years old, or even in his early days with the Government: the intensity born out of his fight for justice that required more than what one person can give on a local level.

Whatever was happening to Merfyn was pointing to his ultimate expression of this justice: to live poverty himself not in an idyllic manner but in a real tangible way. The experience taught him to live and share some ingredients of justice including equal personal relations. A question that faced Merfyn and that should face all persons of faith: how do we live out the faith we have?

Merfyn Temple's memoirs show this great journey, where each step brought satisfaction but also frustration. But he went on devising new ways to continue with the fight. When I met up with him in London in 2007, he was full of stories of how he continued with the fight even as he was the far side of 80 years. Clearly, he had left his heart and soul in Zambia.

Shimwaayi Muntemba
Gender Team, Africa Region
World Bank, Washington DC

From the Editors

As Merfyn's eldest daughter, helping to edit his autobiography has been an intriguing journey into the past. His evocative style of writing has brought to life the shadowed memories of my African childhood and adolescence, which more or less mirror the coming of age of the nation of Zambia, and given them an added lustre. Through this account I have come to understand better what I have inherited, both from him and from the country he loved. I can see that his willingness to listen and learn round the 'camp fire', before taking up arms on behalf of others, often served to temper his headstrong spirit. My experience of growing up with him during those interesting years has been enriched by seeing them again through his eyes, and I am grateful for the gift.

Ruth Quine

A mutual friend passed on Merfyn's contact in the summer of 1986, when our family was looking for an organic farm to work on. Our friendship was forged around endless leek seedlings and bales of spoilt hay. I have been privileged to know and learn from a remarkable man.

My special thanks go to Ruth Quine, for her masterful reduction of the boxes of Merfyn's letters and papers into this crisp narrative, and for her painstaking proof-reading. I have not been much more than the painter on the house she built. Also thanks to John Young, John Pritchard and Colin Morris for their comments and their supply of additional material.

A note on some of Merfyn's remarks from his early years in Northern Rhodesia—a time in Africa very different from the present. Merfyn's earlier attitudes are recorded here in all their unregenerate paternalism. If their colonial tone might offend some of the readers of 2010, not without justification, then the contrast of his radical opinions of later years is all the more remarkable.

Roland Lubett

Preface

I am sitting at the round table at the upstairs window of my new Abbey-field Home. I look down on the busy High Street of Honiton and out to the green fields of Devon's Blackdown Hills.

At my elbow, in many large boxes, is a jumble of documents which span most of the ninety years of my life. There are diaries, letters to my mother, photographs, and an account of my time as a traditional mission-ary on the Nambala mission station in Zambia.

Then comes the drama of my challenge to Colonialism and joining Kenneth Kaunda's United National Independence Party, and my appoint-ment as a civil servant in the newly established Land Resettlement Board. Perhaps the most significant part of my missionary career came when I went to live for eight years with Zambia's poor in the village of Chipapa.

Although I left Africa in 1974, my long association with Zambia con-tinues to this day. The story of my travels with 'The Prayer For Peace', organic agriculture, my ministry in England and my current fundraising to provide secondary school education for AIDS orphans in Zambia, will hopefully be told in volume 2 of my memoirs.

My thanks are due to: my four children who have been such a wonder-ful help to me; Roland Lubett for his sensitive editing of all this material; his daughter Tania for her inspired drawings; Deborah Holland for her striking cover design; and many others including Debbie, my indefatiga-ble typist, and all who helped with proof-reading and comments.

'Stanhope',
36 High Street,
Honiton EX14 1PJ
Tel: 01404 44313
Email: merfyn@tempulu.plus.com

Prologue

MY GREAT-UNCLE WILLIAM BARROWCLOUGH was only twenty-one when he sailed for Sierra Leone, as a missionary of the Wesleyan Methodist Missionary Society. William records that they weighed anchor on Saturday 17 November 1855. He was unable to start his journal until 27 November because of continual sea-sickness.

The diary begins in careful copper-plate:

November 27th 1855 On board the Barque *Dahlia*, at sea not far from Madeira, 27th November 1855. In commencing this journal, I pray that God will help me to be honest with myself, and truthful in all I write, that His glory may be my aim and His grace my assistance.

Nov 28th, 32°32″N, 14°8″W. 28 days distance. At service this evening in the cabin I enlarged upon the doctrine of a particular providence. Gave the steward my little Bible, which I think he will use. Wrote his name in the beginning with the words of Revelation 2:4-5: '...you do not love me now as you did at first. Think how far you have fallen! ...Turn from your sins and do what you did at first.' Went into the hold today, and brought up some pretty spars from among the ballast.

Nov 30th Weather squally, and myself not very well. Have been disappointed of calling at Fouchal Bay for fruits. Finished Cowper's Poetical Works. Subject at Evening service 'Evil of Pride'.

Dec 5th 29°19″N, 16°47″W. working to windward. Thankful for good health again. Mr Dolan (the mate) somewhat better. Gave him some tracts and preserves, and talked seriously with him.

Dec 7th Fasted this morning till one pm and in consequence was weak and ill. Was very desirous of being rightly guided in this thing, so as to obey the command of my Saviour, and at the same time avoid all motives of self-righteousness. Text at Evening Service Ezek. 33:11.

Dec 8th The people came to the captain at noon and had a considerable stir with him about the allowances of sugar and other provisions. The chief mate declared to me this evening seriously, that if I had not been on board, he is sure there would have been murder done. Who can fathom the depths of Providence?

Dec 9th Held service this morning on the quarter deck. This enabled the officer on watch and the man at the wheel to hear. I cannot complain of inattention on the part of my congregation, but it is rather a task to be precentor as well as preacher. I had serious conversation with Wm. Harvey (the unruly spirit). I pray to be made useful to these seafaring men.

Dec 16th, 18°N, 19°20″W. 84 miles. In consequence of some unpleasantness between the captain and mate, the Evening Service was somewhat delayed and at last we had only reading and prayer with the carpenter and steward.

Dec 24th Sierre Leone [*sic*]. Rose early. Packed all up and left the Barque *Dahlia* at about 8 am.

The story told in the journal was very commonplace; but the writing, which began in such perfect copperplate in November 1855, by March 1856 is an untidy scrawl and breaks off in mid-sentence. William Barrowclough had achieved his aim of being a missionary and living his life to the glory of God. He never returned to England, for he died four months later of fever in Bathurst.[1]

---

1 600 miles northwest from Sierra Leone, Bathurst at the mouth of the Gambia River was a Wesleyan mission outpost from 1821. Now renamed Banjul, it is the capital of The Gambia.

Planted in Methodist Soil

I WAS BORN IN WIMBLEDON, the second of four brothers, while my parents were on furlough from missionary work in China. It was my mother who chose the name Merfyn and made sure that the local registrar of births spelt it with an *f*, pointing out to him that all good Welsh people always pronounce it as *v*. Her brother Jack, who knew our Welsh ancestry, said "You can't do that! He might turn out to be a poet."

I was given my second name, Morley, after the doctor who ran the hospital in China where my mother was sent as a young nurse in 1913. She had her own room in the hospital, and when my father in his courting days came up the Yangtze to visit her, he stayed in the guest room attached to the missionary's house. Naturally he wanted to spend as much time as possible with the woman who had smitten him, but at nine o'clock Doctor Morley would stand outside the door and cough discreetly, indicating that it was time for my father to depart for the guest room.

My parents lived on the mission-station at Shiu Chow, now known as Shaoguan, in Guangdong province. They had two colleague couples, Dr and Mrs Hooker, and Dr and Mrs Early, whom they never dreamed of calling by their Christian names. As my mother would say, quoting an old Arab proverb: "If you would keep your hearts together, keep your tents apart."

Few memories remain of my first three years in China. I had a nurse-girl, or *amah*, who called me Ah-Lock. I also remember attending a nursery school, sitting with the other children on a straw mat on the floor, only summoning my mother when I needed her to blow my nose. However, the boat trips home to England, first across the Pacific on the *Empress of*

Australia and then across the Atlantic on the *S.S. Montcalm,* were wonder-fully exciting, as was the three-day train journey across Canada. My father took me up to the front of the train at the station, where they hitched another engine to cross the Rockies. As we waited there, a man came by selling golden ice-cream in a cornet so huge that I needed both hands to hold it.

My Uncle Will's farm

When we got back to England we went to stay at Uncle Will's big wheat farm at Cranswick near Driffield in Yorkshire, while we waited for the Missionary Society to give my father his first appointment. My Uncle Will and Aunt Gertrude had no children of their own, but they seemed to have no problem in accommodating all of us.

It was harvest time, a cloudless day in August 1924, and we were all out in the big seventy-acre field, the workers and myself the four-year-old boy. In one corner of the field was Uncle Will sharpening the small steel blades of the reaper. The foreman, Tom Sawden, sat on the iron sprung seat of the binder, which was drawn by six Shire horses, while Jack the farmer's boy sat astride the right-hand leading mare. The noise was deafening as the binder went clattering by, its eight great wooden sails bending down the tall wheat in the path of the chattering cutters. Miracu-lously they were gathered into sheaves, and the great machine tied them with sisal string snaking from the lid of the red box at Tom's feet. I sat entranced as the binder came by, spewing out an endless line of sheaves as it disappeared into the far distance of my uncle's field.

By ten o'clock the men were tired of the heavy work of building the sheaves into stooks, and they sat down on the golden wheat waiting for their "lowance'. Through the gate came Auntie Gertrude and the fore-man's wife, one carrying a huge enamel canister of tea and mugs, the other with two large baskets of pie and cakes, all covered with a white linen cloth. Sitting on a sheaf beside me was Tom who showed me how to hold out my cup for the steaming tea. It was far too hot to drink, but Tom immediately saw my problem, and taking a penknife from his pocket, he cut a long straw from the sheaf on which we sat and showed me how to sip my tea in comfort.

When the sheaves had dried out in the sun, the time came to 'lead' the corn into the farmyard to be built up in straw stacks. But first each

Merfyn, John, David and Jim

sheaf had to be lifted on a pitchfork up to the stacker on the wagon. When we had finished, I was allowed to take the reins and guide the two horses through the gate on the field edge, and woe betide anyone who knocked down the gatepost with the protruding hub of the wagon's gaily painted front wheel.

I visited my Uncle Will's farm every year, usually at harvest time, but sometimes in spring. I learned to love the sweet smell of dung from the stables and especially in the fold yard where all the rich odours of chicken, cow and pig mixed generously together. Tom taught me how to handle a pitch fork, using it to fill with muck the one-horse 'rully' (cart). He showed me how to yoke old Daisy into the shafts and drive out to spread it on the fields. The art of the game was to stand steady on the swaying heap and twist the fork in your hand so that the muck splayed out evenly over the stubble.

My uncle seemed to spend more time driving to Driffield to get the blacksmith to come out to repair the binder than he did sharpening the cutter blades in the harvest fields. In later years, I also seemed to spend a lot of time under the reaper with spanner and wrench, fixing chains and cogs. Once I showed Tom my bleeding knuckles and all he said was, "Got a bit of bark off."

Early homes in England

After staying with Uncle Will, we went to live in a small house in Bramley, near Dorking. Not far away was a tannery; when the wind blew in our direction it filled the house with unimaginable smells, not unlike the smell from the chicken house at the end of our garden where my father kept his bantams and three Rhode Island Reds for their eggs.

My Aunt Olive, my mother's sister, once came to stay with us and bought a donkey which she kept on the piece of waste ground between us and the tannery. It was an odd thing to do, but perhaps she was thinking back to the days of her childhood when their father owned a donkey-cart; he used to take the cart for services in the village chapels and to visit his church members.

From Bramley, we moved back to Wimbledon. I remember my father taking me up Wimbledon Hill to the Squirrel School for five- and six-year-olds. Tony Gibson and I would sit on the luggage carriers of our fathers' bicycles; my father's was a Rudge Whitworth and his was a Raleigh. Before we reached the top of the hill my father had to dismount, but not so Tony, whose father had fitted a small petrol engine to the back wheel of his bike.

Now with four children on her hands, my mother had little time to give to the religious education of her two eldest boys, so we were sent off on Sunday afternoons to be given lessons by Tony's father, a very erudite minister who did his best for me. However my only memory of that time is of colouring paper camels with wax crayons, then cutting them out, putting them on paper stands, and moving them across the sand tray which Mr Gibson had devised to teach us the basic stories of the Old Testament.

During these years, my father was effectively on deputation for the Missionary Society. However when I was about seven years old, we moved to Truro in Cornwall, to take up a congregational appointment.

My mother, Ruth Barrowclough

My mother's Uncle Owen and Aunt Elizabeth had six children: Charles, Owen, Elsie, Margaret, Lilian and Lucie, none of whom married. The six lived together in an enormous house on Hampstead Heath called 'The Logs'. They were so very rich, those cousins of my mother. None of them ever had to work. Charles spent his whole life playing with his chemistry set which filled the basement of The Logs. Owen and Lilian gave their lives to voluntary good works, mostly at the Leysian Mission in the East End of London, though in spring and summer they would visit Cwm Rhaider, their large Welsh sheep farm in the hills above Machynlleth.

One day, Lilian and Lucie took their young cousin, my elder brother John, to Hamleys, the famous toy shop in Regent Street. "You can have anything you like," they told him. John wandered around the fabulous shelves and then said modestly that he would like a set of tin soldiers costing just one shilling and nine pence. At this point Lilian and Lucie, who had been deeply impressed by this polite, well-spoken boy, decided that he should not be allowed to attend the local council school in Truro; he must be sent to the great Methodist public school, The Leys, in Cambridge, where their brothers Charles and Owen had been educated under the wise tutelage of Dr Barber, a Methodist minister. 'The Logs', as we came to call our cousins, were so impressed by the steady progress of their surrogate son John that they ended up sending all four of us Temple boys to The Leys.

My mother's father and grandfather were both Wesleyan ministers, and according to the rules of Methodism of that time, did not receive a stipend, but were given an allowance in addition to the house, which every circuit provided. All the furnishings—carpets, curtains, bed sheets, cutlery and crockery—were the responsibility of the circuit steward and his wife. I sometimes wonder what it was like for my grandmother, sister of the proprietor of Owen Owen's department store, to go cap in hand to ask for a new carpet to replace the one in the hall made threadbare by her predecessors' feet, or for a new mattress for her bed, or a new mangle for the outhouse. Our family was in the same position, and I remember my mother's relief when she escaped from the rather niggardly stewards of Cornwall into the more generous hands of the affluent congregation in Cambridge.

My mother early taught me the value of money. From the age of seven, I was sent down to the greengrocer at the bottom of Mitchell Hill, to buy some item she had forgotten when doing the shopping herself. Once

I kept tuppence to buy myself a paper cone of toffees, but my mother quickly discovered my misdemeanour. There was no row, no smack, no sending me off to my room, but there was such disapproval in her eye that I never stole again. She was for me the great provider of everything that mattered in my life: my clothes, my friends, my food and all my outings to the seaside.

My mother always kept her accounts in the greatest detail, and must have worked out that it cost her about ninepence a day to buy our food, so one day she gave me nine pennies and told me to look after myself. I cannot remember now what I spent the money on, but when my friend Jimmy Thompson invited me out to tea that day, I told his mother I couldn't eat anything; not even my favourite dish called 'thunder and lightning', which consisted of mixing Tate & Lyle's golden syrup with Cornish butter or clotted cream, then spreading it generously on thick slices of brown bread. Such was my total obedience to my mother's words.

She had bought a Citroën car, primarily for my father's use so that he could go out to visit his people in the villages and preach there on Sundays, but during the week my mother, who had taught herself to drive, would take her four boys out to play on the sands of Perranporth, Veryan, Holywell, or Newquay. At that time the beaches were empty of people, and there were not many cars on the road. I think I knew just about all of them: Citroën, Jowett, bull-nosed Morris Cowley, Hillman, and my flamboyant Uncle Jack's Alitalia. Someone, I think it was jokey Uncle Fred, told me to keep my eyes open for a 'Bamboosler'. No one ever told me that there was no such car, and for years I searched for it in vain.

Although I never heard my parents talk about their faith, except when we said grace before meals and when my father offered a prayer for 'journeying mercies' before we left for school, it shone through in their love for us. When I went away to school, my mother gave me a little book with a soft green leather cover called 'Daily Light'. The verse of scripture for 7 November, my birthday, was Romans 5:3 and I determined to learn it by heart, which meant waiting till the candle was put out and taking the book down illegally to the bottom of my bed to read by torchlight. I had no idea what it meant. How could a child understand what *tribulation worketh patience* might mean? Only seventy-five years later would I truly understand.

Our parents set out the rules that we were expected to keep until we reached the magic age of twenty-one: no gambling, no smoking, no drinking of alcoholic beverages and no playing cards on Sundays. There was obligatory attendance at Sunday worship, where I sat beside my mother, always listening to the children's address, then sitting silently through the long sermons, licking the rabbit-fur collar of her Sunday best winter coat. I was not allowed to attend Sunday School because, as I once heard my mother say to her sister Olive, "Do they think I would entrust my children's religious education to some tuppenny ha'penny servant girl?"

Not only did my mother take our religious education into her own hands, but she also thought it necessary to make us self-reliant and fully aware of what was going on around us. For example, when out on our long walks with my elder brother John, we were taught to name the flowers and trees in the hedgerows. "This is the petal and this the sepal, this is the stamen and this the pistil. This is an oak, a beech, an ash. This is a sycamore from which you can make a whistle and this is a hazel whose sapling you can cut down to make a spear. When you are hungry in the early spring you can nibble the fresh green leaves of hawthorn. You can take a sweet chestnut home to cook on the sitting room fire, but never a conker."

On the other side of the manse in Truro, behind a high brick wall, was the Council School. Sometimes I would swing on the garden gate and watch the children down the road come streaming out of school. In groups of three or four they would call out to me, probably asking why I was not in class with them. I never said much in reply, perhaps because I could not understand their broad Cornish accents, but more likely because I did not want to tell them that I went to Miss Philips' Dame School in the front room of a very large house in Jubilee Crescent. When it was discovered that I had been swinging on the garden gate, I was strictly forbidden to go down there when the local children were coming out of school.

I cannot imagine growing up in any home happier than ours, for though my mother was seen by her nephews and nieces as strict, she was very kind and generous to us. Once a week, between supper and bed-time, the house was closed to all callers. We children stripped naked and were allowed to rush up and down the stairs and in and out of all the rooms. We were allowed to sing and dance and shout to our heart's content, but not so loudly that our neighbours might hear us.

Determined in her heart that all her four sons would become mission-aries, my mother made sure that the books she read to us before we went to bed, were 'missionary books'. There was *John Williams: The Shipbuilder* who, when shipwrecked off some island in the Southern Seas, with axe and adze hewed the logs and built himself a boat in which he escaped. There was *James Chalmers: The Great Heart of Papua*, who was killed and eaten by cannibals. Best of all was *David Livingstone: The Pathfinder*. Each book had a picture on the cover. I remember gazing up from the floor beside my mother's chair at the figure of David Livingstone fending off with his gun a leaping lion. Somehow he survived, but his right shoulder always bore the marks of this assault.

My father, John Temple

When my father was at Dids-bury College in Manchester he met Douglas Gray, and they both became members of what was called The Missionary Platform. I think it was here that my father was deeply influenced by the call to offer himself as a missionary. At that time, to become a mission-ary was regarded by the church as being the zenith of Christian ser-vice. For my father's generation, the challenge of taking the gospel of Christ to 'heathen lands afar' was both mysterious and romantic. My parents inherited the great romantic sentiments of the Victorians.

In 1910 my father was appointed by the Wesleyan Methodist Missionary Society to China, and his friend Douglas to Africa. During the First World War, my father went to the front line on the Western Front as chaplain to the troops. He rarely mentioned the War, but once, when we were talk-ing together about the sacrament of Holy Communion, he told me that the troops were not much bothered when he administered the sacrament behind the lines. However, when they were in the trenches together and the time came for them to 'go over the top', it had a much deeper significance.

Sometimes my mother, who always got up early to get the breakfast, would allow us to snuggle up with father in the double bed. That was when he told us stories about his early days in China, especially about the 'brigands'. He was never captured himself, though he told stories of his missionary friends who were. There was one who was stripped of everything including his Bible. He asked to have it back since it was his most treasured possession, but they refused, except to allow him to tear out one book. Whether because it was the last and the easiest to take, I do not know, but he tore out the Book of Revelation.

To me as a child of seven, my father seemed to have spent most of his time escaping from brigands. But I remember one story about how he called on a local mandarin, at the time when he was only beginning to learn Chinese. He enquired tenderly about this man's wives. He was taken aback when the mandarin replied, "Very well thank you, but I had to kill a couple yesterday." When my father had his next Chinese lesson, he repeated his enquiry and asked his teacher whether the mandarin's wives had really come to their gruesome end. His mentor smiled and said, "You didn't say wives, you said goats."

Other stories were about his journeys up-country. He slept in the rat-infested village inns. When he put the lantern out, the rats moved in, and he had to sleep with his head under the blanket lest they bit off his ear. At one point on the journey he came to a deep river with high banks. As no one seemed to be around, he stripped naked and dived off the high bank. Unbeknown to him some women were washing their clothes in the water below. When he came hurtling from the sky above, they rushed away to tell their friends that they had seen a naked *gwai lo* or 'foreign devil'.

In the Truro days you might say I hardly knew my father. He was a kind and loving figure hovering in the background of my life, appearing now and again to give us a special treat like a bottle of pop or an ice-cream. On one occasion it was to administer justice to me with a slap on the hand from my mother's long-handled hairbrush. My elder brother was three years older, but I was a pugnacious little boy, and after a quarrel in which I threw him down to the bottom of the stairs, my father came out of his study and rightly took his side in the affair. That was about the only time I incurred his wrath.

My father, having married a very strongly-principled wife, usually left the discipline of their children in her hands. However, on one occasion

my youngest brother David, aged five, had been dropped off at his school on the other side of town. We had no telephone then, but somehow he heard that David had been seen climbing along the railings on the high wall above the railway station. My father jumped into the car and dashed off to rescue him. On returning to the house he said to my elder brother John, "What shall we do with David?"

"Tell him he is a silly ass and take him back to school," said John.

That was how brother John was and continued to be until he died: always strict, prosaic, down to earth, and immensely caring of others' needs.

Sometimes at table my parents would enter into what we felt were animated arguments, for they were both highly intelligent and intensely aware people. We children sometimes became rather upset and would say, "Why do you argue so much?" and they would reply, "We are not arguing, we are discussing." Of course they were right, for there was nothing personal about their disagreements; each had their own views and held each other in the greatest respect.

When we sat at the breakfast table discussing what to do that day, the phrase so often on my father's lips was, "This is liberty hall—use your own judgment, my boys, and it won't take you long to discover your mistakes." He always had our best interests at heart and knew how to work quietly behind the scenes to make things happen for our benefit.

I remember one occasion when we set out in a snowstorm. About a mile from the village to which we were going, the Citroen sank to its axles in the snow. We carried on by foot, we small children making heavy weather of it in the deep snow; however it did not hold my father back. He hurried on ahead to get to the chapel by 10.30 and told us not to worry because if we followed in his footsteps we would make it—true in every sense.

In my teenage years we had our differences, because I found him to be a great supporter of traditional values, while I considered myself a pacifist and a revolutionary. As war with Germany loomed, my father thought Hitler and the Nazis should be opposed at all costs, whereas I saw it all as the consequence of the ill-treatment of the Germans after the 1914-18 war. But whatever our disagreements, he remained unwavering in his support, and our relationship remained as strong as ever.

Among my Truro memories, one stands out beyond all others. One day my father announced that his old college chum Douglas Gray was coming on deputation to his church. "People call Douglas Gray 'the modern Livingstone of Africa'," said my father, "because he too was leapt on by a leopard whose claw all but severed his jugular vein."

How can I forget that summer evening? I stood on the steps of the manse, a seven-year-old boy holding his father by the hand. We heard the front gate click, then saw a short wiry man with jet-black hair come striding up the gravel path to our front door. Before he could set foot in our house, I said, "Please, can I see the scar?"

"Well, not at the moment," he said, "but if you'd like to come upstairs to the bathroom, I'll show it to you." He told me that the incident had happened about two years before, but the scar was still a vivid red where the leopard's claws had ripped his flesh. So began my romance with Africa, and my dream of becoming a missionary.

After four years in Truro, my father was invited to be the 'second minister' in Cambridge with responsibility for the Methodist students there. I have never discovered quite how this invitation came about, because my father was no academic, and one would have expected such an influential job to go to someone with a degree. Within a quarter of a mile of the manse was Wesley College, one of the smallest of the five Methodist col-

leges, with only about 25 students, because they were all expected to leave
with a good Cambridge degree. On one occasion my father had been talking to the students, saying, "All you students when you leave college will
expect to be given the plum jobs in Methodism." One of them, Irvonwy
Morgan, came to my father some time later, having taken his words to
heart, and said he did not want a plum job; he wanted a real and difficult
job. My father suggested he go to the East End Mission, on the Isle of
Dogs in East London. Irvonwy Morgan served in the East End for the next
forty years of his life.

My mother called that year in Cambridge her *annus mirabilis*, and I
think was silently disappointed when my father became one of two secretaries at the British and Foreign Bible Society. One was an Anglican under
whose care would fall the Near East, Africa, India and Central Asia, while
my father as Free Churchman covered the rest: Europe, North and South
America, and of course China, the most populous country in the world.

The coming of World War II gave my father a special opportunity
to exercise his charm among the members of the refugee governments
based in London. The impression he created may be judged by the hon-
ours bestowed on him by the King of Norway and the Queen of Holland. Perhaps even better evidence was the honour given him after the
war, when at the Elfinsward Conference in May 1946, by unanimous vote
he was invited to become the first General Secretary of the United Bible
Societies.[1]

Sadly John Temple did not long survive the birth of the UBS. On a
journey to his beloved China in 1948, he died and is buried in Hong Kong.
My mother received letters from around the world; perhaps the one which
most faithfully described him came from Bishop Bergrav in Norway who
said, "John Temple had the sun in him."

---

1 John Temple had seen the strategic opportunity for translation and promulgation of the Scriptures—a "peace dividend"—and convened the Conference, inviting the American, Dutch and
a number of other national bible societies, together with the British and Foreign Bible Society,
to found the UBS.

Wrestling with School

In 1927, at the age of eight and three-quarters, the time came for me to follow my brother John to boarding school at Earnseat in Arnside, Westmoreland.

Why were we sent to a school at the other end of England? My parents, knowing that their four sons were destined for The Leys public school, had to find the best preparatory school in the country. My father consulted the headmaster of The Leys, a fellow-minister, who said, "I receive boys from all over England and Wales and I have to deal with any number of preparatory schools. There is one which I consider to be the best in the country. It is called Earnseat in Westmoreland. I suggest you send your sons there."

Some years earlier the headmaster of this school, Jimmy Barnes, had bought two adjacent houses on the sea-front of the little town of Arnside. Here the fifty boys slept at night, ate their food and played together in the book-lined common room; and we had our lessons every day in Ashmeadow, the big house at the end of the promenade. I never knew the name of Jimmy's wife because we all called her 'Mum B', and what an amazing woman she was, with three children of her own and an apparently limitless love for every one of the children in her husband's school. She ran the whole domestic establishment with diminutive Sarah, her trusted senior housemaid, two other housemaids and young Tommy, the boot-boy and odd-job man, who could turn his hand to anything.

Going back and forth from Arnside to Truro was a two-day train journey; we had to stay overnight in London, where my uncle was a dentist in Welbeck Street. I remember he used to take us to Fleming's Café. When

John was fourteen and I was eleven, my mother arranged for us to travel down the East Coast from Hull to Truro on a cargo ship. I think there were only six passengers: four men and ourselves. I imagine the ship travelled mostly at night, putting in at various ports along the way. There was endless entertainment as we watched the sailors handle the cargo out of the hold, using a winch and rope attached to a sloping spar with a rattling pulley at the top. My mother saw all this as part of our education for life, and I suppose we were expected to learn the names of the ports at which we called and what kind of cargo was being shipped, but we were far too excited to record such things.

Nobody knows I am dyslexic

My days at school in Earnseat were some of the happiest in my life, but I caused much worry to my parents. This is revealed in the series of letters they received three times a year from Jimmy Barnes, which indicate why, compared with their eldest son's progress in his lessons, their second son was far behind.

> *5 Jan 1929*: "Dear Mr and Mrs Temple, I hope we shall not spoil 'secundus' at Earnseat for he is undoubtedly a boy of unusually attractive and likeable temperament and disposition. The only 'but' in the case is that he is distinctly backward in reading and spelling and almost painfully slow with writing and work generally."
>
> *4 August 1930*: "Mr Daw (3rd teacher) tells me he has been disconcerted by Merfyn's inability to be accurate in written work. The result gives one the impression of carelessness, but I am not sure how far it is under his own control. He will spell the same word quite differently on consecutive lines and sometimes seems quite unable to copy work from the board without numerous mistakes. I hope it is only a temporary phase as such a habit (if it becomes habitual) would be very detrimental to future progress. It is just possible that the summer term affords too many distractions out of doors and Merfyn finds it difficult to concentrate sufficiently on indoor studies."
>
> *9th August 1932*: "Taffy, I am afraid, in the narrow and limited academic sphere is going to be something of a problem (Taffy was the name I was given, because they knew I was of Welsh origin). Of the nineteen boys in Form IV he definitely falls into the bottom group of three or four in all subjects. It is not easy to see how he is ever going to stand up to examination

tests with any real credit. He is simply not the intellectual type. And yet there is no jollier, happier, more sociable, more likeable boy at Earnseat than he."

There is clear indication here of my dyslexia. Although Jimmy Barnes had not heard of the term, he was a good enough educator to realise that something was wrong.

From Latin to landscaping

Fortunately for me, Earnseat laid little store by academic excellence. One summer evening when I was all alone in the classroom of Ashmeadow, being kept in after school to rewrite a passage of translation from Caesar's *Gallic Wars*, Jimmy Barnes walked in and glanced over my shoulder.

"Taffy," he said, "I don't think, however long we keep you in, you will ever be able to translate from the Latin. I've got a little job for you to do. You know that sloping ground which goes up from the lawn into the plantation? Well it's becoming tangled with brambles. Take this pruning knife and these gloves, and cut the brambles out at their roots." Which I did, not only that summer evening, but every day until every single bramble root had been cut.

School projects

At the beginning of each summer term, Jimmy announced some new project he had thought up for developing our practical abilities. One was the model railway. Somehow he had become friends with Josiah Stamp, the head of the LMS[1], who gave Jimmy £50 for a model railway project. We laid the line in the plantation, assembling rails and sleepers, digging cuttings and using an old railway sleeper to cross a gully. We had all the rolling stock we needed and there was enough money left over to buy two Bassett-Lowke steam engines.

The Second Master, Pa Wright, taught not only his own class but also mathematics throughout the school. He must have found me well-nigh impossible to teach, because I frequently put numbers in the wrong order, especially when figures were above a thousand. However, he also taught me geometry; I became quite good with a set square and ruler, and once

---

1 Josiah Stamp, 1st Baron Stamp, was a British civil servant, industrialist, economist, statistician and banker. He was a director of the Bank of England and chairman of the London Midland and Scottish Railway.

got a mark of 10 out of 10. When we went out one day on the lawn in Ashmeadow to mark out the oval running track with white lime, he showed me the beauty of a 'three, four, five' right-angled triangle. If I learned nothing else from Pa Wright, I shall always be grateful for Pythagoras' theorem, for I never made a mistake when marking out a building's foundations.

Echoes of the War

For at least four afternoons a week, when it was not raining, Pa Wright would take us for walks on the Knott, or to Fairy Steps, or to the ruined watchtower. At one place, which we called the Pine Forest despite the fact that the only trees were yews, we were allowed to climb the trees and gather sticks to make platforms as do chimpanzees. At another, where there was a scree of small flat stones, we built little fairy houses. Often for an hour or two in the middle of our walk we were allowed to play 'wide games' which involved one team choosing its base camp and the other attacking it. There was much chasing and shouting and dashing about.

Pa Wright never talked very much on these walks, but his terrible experiences during the war had made him a passionate believer in peace, and he was secretary of the Arnside village 'League of the United Nations'. Occasionally he would invite some of the older boys to attend a meeting in the village hall to which various speakers were invited. Who they were I do not know, but this was a time when Britain was frantically disarming under Ramsay Macdonald, and I remember the ripple of disapproval when one speaker quoted Clemenceau's famous axiom 'If you want peace, prepare for war'.

Bird-watching on the marshes

Not only was Jimmy Barnes an amateur naturalist, he was a great bird lover too. On Sunday afternoons, in order to give the Second Master a rest, he would take us for a walk in crocodile. At the beginning of each spring term, any boy over the age of eleven who wished to do so was given an exercise book with four columns: date, time, bird's nest found, and comment. Certain rules were laid down; for example, that we must never steal an egg, and if the bird was sitting we must never disturb it, even though it was likely to fly off when we climbed the tree.

Once in a while, when the weather was glorious, Jimmy Barnes would come into the classroom and announce a holiday. First he had to ring up the stationmaster to make sure that no trains were running, and then we were taken over the railway viaduct which crosses the River Kent to the salt marshes on the other side. When we reached the other side, the whole school fanned out across the marshes to look for baby chicks. When we found one—dunlin, redshank or plover—we signalled to the headmaster or his son, who would come over with their clippers and ring the bird.

Public school: The Leys

I finally scraped through the entrance examinations, and in September 1933 started at The Leys in Cambridge. At a practical level, this was not a problem for me, because my older brother John was already there and he had told me what life was like in a public school.

However, looking back on the few diaries that have survived from this time, I now realise I was in unconscious revolt against my father for sending me to a school which was going to force me to become an academic, the very thing that Jimmy Barnes had warned him against. I was also in revolt against what The Leys stood for. It was a school for the sons of rich parents, and in comparison with them I was poor.

The basic ethos of the school was evident on the chapel walls. The chapel was a memorial to the hundreds of young men who had died in the First World War, their names being inscribed in gilded panels on the walls. The names were also on the outside wall, and here we gathered for the two minutes' silence on Armistice Day. Inscribed on the wall were the words *Dulce et Decorum est pro Patria Mori*: it is sweet and honourable to die for your country. The school was based on the assumption that we were being trained and educated to become the nation's leaders and rulers, and almost everything was done with this end in view.

The Officers' Training Corps

An essential part of this assumption was the Officers' Training Corps (OTC), the cadet force of the school. The key person in the OTC was Sergeant-Major Withers, who had served King and Country through the First World War, showing the scars on his face and hands. He was chosen to teach us how to become leaders.

Everyone must look exactly the same, which means you must dress properly in your army uniform.
1. You must dubbin your boots.
2. You must bandage each leg in a four-foot khaki puttee.
3. You must use a button-stick to polish your brass buttons.
Beyond all else you must learn how to use your rifle and your bayonet.

Sergeant-Major Withers would say, "This is your Lee-Enfield .303 rifle. This is the trigger and the bolt. You have six cartridges in your magazine and when you fire, make sure every bullet finds its mark."

For most of us it was a kind of charade in which we were pretending to be soldiers, for no-one really believed there could be another war. It was also about obeying commands. I can still hear Sergeant-Major Withers' barking voice when we were presenting arms: "When I says 'fix' you don't fix, but when I says 'bayonets' you whips 'em out, whops 'em on and waits awhile." While you waited you remained absolutely still with no movement of your body, head fixed with unblinking eyes looking straight forward into the middle distance, waiting for the next command.

I become a pacifist

At fifteen years old, I found myself thinking about a world outside the narrow confines of our school. I attended meetings of our debating society and the Christian Union after church on Sundays, and began to read copies of the Spectator in the library.

My diary records say: "Lewis and I went to a Peace Meeting at St Andrews' Hall. Canon Raven was in the chair and the speakers were Rev J. S. Whale (Congregationalist) and a Quaker lady whose name was Fry. Whale gave us a broadcast talk which the BBC had not allowed him to give. Very good arguments . . ." Apparently some parents of boys at The Leys had objected to their sons being drafted automatically into the OTC, and a young science teacher called Reg Ayres, himself a pacifist, had started a Scout troop. I went to the master who was commanding the OTC, and told him I wished to resign because I was a pacifist. He argued for a while and then said disdainfully, "Well you had better go and join Mr. Ayres' Scout troop, hadn't you?" Attitudes of non-conformity were already deep inside me. Many years later I was to become a Scout Commissioner in Northern Rhodesia and a dedicated follower of Kenneth Kaunda, who had pledged that his followers would achieve independence non-violently.

An extra year at The Leys

How I managed I shall never know, but in spite of my dyslexia, I scraped through my exam and managed to pass my Matric in all necessary subjects—except Latin. This was a blow to my father who, having left school at the age of fourteen, was deter-mined that every one of his sons should enter life with a university degree. He dis-cussed with me the possi-bility of going into business with Owen Owen's, as he knew he could 'pull strings' there because of his connections through my mother. But it would have raised problems, since it was the Owen family who had paid my fees to go to a public school, and they would not be pleased if one of their protégés had not gone on to university.

Jimmy Barnes was proving right; I simply did not have an academic bone in my body. However, my father was a determined man, and he decided to put his problem to the headmaster of The Leys, who said, "Just keep him on here for another year. I will make him a prefect and we will give him special coaching in Latin to make sure he can sit that subject again."

Perhaps that extra year at school was a good thing, because I was growing up fast and continued to benefit from the powerful influence of two of my schoolmasters. One was Donald Hughes, who taught English. Every week he made us write an essay on current topics such as 'Why I shall vote in the next election' or 'Why it is sometimes right to wage war.'

Above all else he taught me to love poetry. The other was Conrad Skinner the chaplain, who delicately guided me into a deeper understanding of what it means to be a Christian.

I meet Audrey

At seventeen, I went with my brother Jim to help our Uncle Will with the wheat harvest. One day he announced that a girl named Audrey was also coming to stay on the farm. We went in the car to meet her at the station two miles away in Driffield, but she did not arrive as expected. I sat for ages speculating on who this girl might be. All they had told me was her name, Audrey; it was a good name and I liked it. They said she had once lived in Africa, but when she was eight years old her mother had died and she had come to school in England. Then we saw her, a tiny figure caught for a moment in the headlights of the car, a slip of a girl bent sideways as she lugged her bulging suitcase along the winding road.

Uncle Will said the supper which Auntie Gertrude had prepared for us in the farm kitchen must now be cold, so we went back to the fish and chip shop in Driffield. Many times since, as we recalled that day, Audrey would say, "It was against the lighted window of a fish-and-chip shop that I caught my first glimpse of Merfyn's profile and thought, 'He's rather dishy'."

I met Audrey twice more on the farm; her father, Douglas Gray, through my father, was a great friend of Uncle Will's. On one occasion we were hoeing turnips in a five-acre field. Once when we slackened on the job, Tom passed by and shouted, "Give 'em belltinker!" Years later, when I asked about the origin of the word, I was told that in the days when men fought bare-fisted, Bell Tinker was the champion boxer of the East Riding. It was easier to take a breather when we went stooking in the forty-acre field, for what better place is there to snuggle down than in the dim light of a long stook?

Methodist Training College

Having finally managed to pass my Latin exams at The Leys, I was sent by my father to King's College in London to take an arts degree. It was a disaster: I failed in every subject—Latin, French, English and history.

After a year at college, the Principal wrote to my father to say that it would not be possible for me to return. It was then that my father's charm and godly deviousness came into full play. I can see him thinking to himself, "Merfyn doesn't know it yet, but he has it in him to become a good Methodist minister. He needs more time to find this out for himself. I know what to do; I will go and see my friend Dr Ryder Smith, principal of the Methodist Training College at Richmond-on-Thames. I shall ask him to give my son half an hour of his valuable time and tell me what he makes of him." Which he did, and I was accepted.

It was 1938 and we stood on the brink of war. That autumn at the age of nineteen, I was taken in as the only layman in a class of fifty, all of whom were accepted candidates for the Methodist ministry. Perhaps when Dr Smith finally accepted me he was thinking of his young students, many of whom would serve as chaplains and perhaps not return. One never did—my friend Roy Pitkin.

Conversion

It was college practice to divide all the students into class meetings, and every week about twelve of us gathered in each of the houses of the four tutors. I was allocated to Dr Smith's class meeting and we sat in a circle in his sitting room. "We will start tonight," said the Principal, "by each of you giving an account of your religious experience." To the others, this was not a problem, for an account of conversion was one of the conditions of being accepted into the ministry. When my turn came, I sat silent, blushing a deep red in my confusion; I had no idea what a religious experience of conversion was.

This was remedied some time later when one Sunday afternoon I had been to London to hear one of the great Methodist preachers: Soper, Weatherhead or Sangster.[2] My return path led through Trafalgar Square. Big crowds of Communists and anti-Communists were clashing in the streets, and a few police—far too few—had arrived to keep them apart. I saw one mounted policeman being pulled from his horse. He was trying desperately to keep the rioters at bay, while at the same time holding on to the reins of his rearing mount. I had never been caught up in a riot before. It both excited and shocked me, because the air was full of anger as these rival groups cursed and yelled at one another.

2 The great triumvirate of London Methodist preachers of the 1930s. Donald Soper was superintendent of the West London Mission, based at the Kingsway Hall; his friend Leslie Weatherhead was packing in the crowds at the City Temple, and Edwin Sangster was preaching from Central Hall, Westminster. It was said of them that "Sangster loves God, Weatherhead loves the people and Soper loves an argument."

"What are you going to do about it?" I said to myself. "You say you believe in non-violence and that you are a follower of Jesus the Prince of Peace. You had better get up and tell them so. But what are you going to say?"

Jesus said to me, "You don't need to worry about that because I once said to my disciples 'When you don't know what to say I will put words into your mouth'."

I climbed on top of one of the bollards, beneath one of the great stone lions in Trafalgar Square. What I said I do not precisely remember, but a group of rioters gathered round me and sang mockingly, "Tell me the old, old story . . ." They pulled me off my pedestal just as they had done to the policeman on his horse, and I made my way to the edge of the crowd. A man wearing a long mackintosh came up and said, "I come from Switzerland. All the while you were up there I was fingering my rosary and I prayed for you."

I had been given my experience of conversion. It was so simple. Jesus had told me to do something: I had done it. He had done what He said He would do—He had put words into my mouth.

Not joining up

When war finally did break out, nearly all my old school friends joined the army, navy and air force. When my turn came, I decided that I wanted to be a stretcher-bearer, because I needed to be where the action was, but I didn't want to fight. I went down to the local recruiting office and told them my plan. All went well until they said, "The only way to be a stretcher-bearer is to join the Royal Army Medical Corps which is part of the Royal Army Service Corps, and when you join that you will for your own safety carry a rifle."

"I can't agree to that," I said. Then fate stepped in for, in a time when church and state collaborated, all ministers of religion were given the status of 'reserved occupations', so I was exempted from national service.

Romance blooms with Audrey

Every summer at the College, we held a garden party to raise money for overseas missions. I was given the task of running the missionary book-stall and decided to dress up as an Arab to lend colour to the proceedings, even turning my face and hands a gentle brown. I had written to Audrey asking her to come, and I think I was more interested in meeting her again than in selling the books.

It was a perfect summer's day in 1939, and the college lawn was alive with people. From the corner of my eye I saw her coming, dressed in a frock of pale blue with a small white collar and pretty white buttons. The girl I had last seen in Uncle Will's harvest field was now a woman. When all the festivities were over I took her up to my room where we saw another view of our beautiful college grounds still dappled with sunlight in the cool of the evening. Standing there together, hardly talking, we felt something pass between us for the first time.

When Audrey was at school, she had bought an ancient lady's bicycle with brightly-coloured cord laced between small holes in the back mudguard and the bracket above the hub. She called it 'Wilberforce' and loved it dearly. Once I cleaned it for her and painted the rusty rims a golden yellow, but she did not approve and I had to paint them black again. I had also bought for myself, for £1 in a second-hand shop on Richmond Bridge, an ex-policeman's bicycle in tip-top condition; it even had a Sturmey-Archer three-speed gear.

One spring weekend in 1940, Audrey had come to stay in our family home in Beckenham where, for safety from air raids, she slept in the broom cupboard under the stairs. The next day we set off on our bicycles to explore the woods between Farnborough and Downe. I wanted to show off my knowledge of birds; however there was one whose song I could not identify—but suddenly, there it was, sitting in the branches of a young oak tree. It was a chaffinch, and he seemed to have come from the forest just to sing for us. We flung ourselves down amongst the wood anemones and the bluebells, ate our picnic, pledged our troth and cycled back home to tell the world that we were now engaged.

A holiday job

After a year at college mixing with a wide range of students from many walks of life, I was beginning to hear of a world very different from the one I had experienced at my public school. When the summer holidays came, I announced to my parents that I was off to see that world for myself. I told myself I must do what Jesus had told his disciples to do: "do not carry any gold, silver, or copper money in your pockets . . . or extra shirt or shoes or a walking stick." (Matthew 10: 9-10)

The story of that experience was published in the college magazine under the title 'Casual Labour':

"Charlie! Wake up lad." Charlie rubbed his eyes, and tumbled out of bed. Whose voice was that? For a moment he couldn't remember where he was; then suddenly it all came back to him and, as he clambered into his dusty clothes in the dim light of that little room, the events of the last two days flashed through his mind like some broken dream. The first excitement of leaving behind his old life, which he had known for nineteen years, and the thrill of the open road, the challenge of the unknown; then pavements, endless pavements, loneliness, the cold night hours as he lay on the slatted bench on the embankment looking out over the Thames; the kindly little man who asked whether it was a broken love affair that sent him away from home; the policeman who stopped him to search his little sack of belongings; the first struggle with the pride that welled within his breast forbidding him to beg a lift from the lorries on the road, tired feet, the ache which was still there when the last crumb of his one dry crust had gone. The sun low down on the horizon, nowhere to sleep, nothing to eat, no money, then Bill the lorry driver with his mouth full of oaths and his heart full of kindness, who found him a job in a brick-yard and gave him food and a bed for the night.

It was not a dream after all; there was that voice again and it was Bill's: "Hurry up, Charlie," reinforced with numerous expletives. He had just time to snatch the bottle of cold tea put out for him on the kitchen table, and stuffing a packet of tomato sandwiches into his pocket, dash out to where Bill was waiting on his motorcycle. It was after half past five, they had to be at work at six, but Bill knew how to drive and Charlie loved that mad ride early in the morning with the wind streaming through his hair. The little foreman in his dirty dungarees showed him where he was to work. It was a simple job, a soul-destroying job; for twelve long hours he stood before a great machine which turned out bricks, bricks, bricks, in a never-ending line. He lifted them and stacked them on a barrow which was emptied every now and then by men damp with sweat from working in the sweltering kilns. For a week he worked side by side with those men; they never understood him, but during the long night shift when the hours crawled by like years, they cheered him with a smile for they knew 'his back was aching and his hands were not yet hardened'. He sat with them in the canteen, gulped down mugs full of boiling tea, watched them eat and doze and swear and snigger.

He saw life, an ugly, sprawling, naked thing, shorn of all those conventions which veil the passions of men. At first he hated it all but realised that what he looked upon with loathing was life for these men. Before he lived with them he called it sin, but when he saw them sweating in those stifling kilns, when he heard them laugh and wondered what they found to laugh about in the drabness of homes and lodging houses, he knew that all the guilt was not theirs; they had souls but they were tiny undeveloped things. These men were nurtured in a hard and unforgiving world; they were children of an age which gave them no chance to express their own God-given natures except through their native instincts. Charlie came away saddened, but more sure than ever that Christ came that men might have life and have it more abundantly.

Waiting for the ship

By the summer of 1941 my studies were complete and I was an ordained minister. Although I had been appointed by the Methodist Missionary Society to Northern Rhodesia, I had to wait with all my boxes packed until the War Office could tell me of a ship ready to sail to Cape Town. While I waited, my father pulled the necessary strings and arranged for me to be appointed as a probationer to a bombed-out church in Lewisham. Attached to Lewisham

was the little church of Brockley. I was invited over on a Saturday to conduct a wedding and at the small reception afterwards met some of the guests, a few of whom had come from far away and had stayed in the bride's house overnight. That evening the German bombers came and the house was totally destroyed. As I was the last person to see the occupants alive, the police asked me to go over to identify them in the morgue. I had never seen a dead body before, and that night I couldn't sleep.

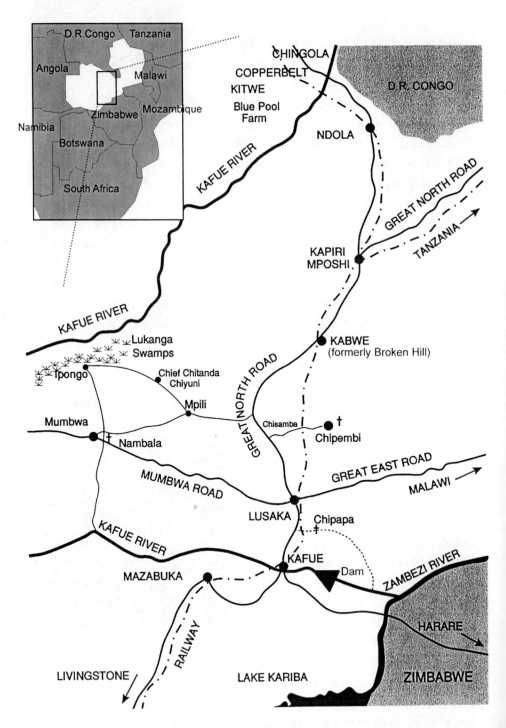

Central Zambia

First Steps into Africa

AT LAST THE LONG-AWAITED TELEGRAM came from the War Office, and I took my leave. It was hard for my parents to say goodbye, but they had been missionaries themselves, and so they would understand. As for me, my heart was being torn apart. Of course I had been called to serve God as a missionary—there was no doubt about that—but why did I have to leave my beloved behind? I felt the Missionary Society was being unfair to me, in enforcing their draconian rule which stated "At no time during his seven years' probationary period may a missionary marry."

It was not until two years later at a Missionary Conference held at Chalimbana in Northern Rhodesia that I found the words which would adequately express my feelings. There I met a recently married young man sent out by the Church of Scotland called George Frazer, who having heard my story, just said, "That's bloody, really bloody." I did not think that missionaries knew how to swear like that.

I set sail on a cargo ship for Cape Town. There were eighty passengers, but we had little space on the deck, which was piled high with huge packing cases containing the wings and fuselage of Spitfires being sent out for pilot training in Southern Rhodesia. When we left Liverpool we travelled in a great convoy, with ships in all directions as far as the eye could see, and it was not until we reached the entrance to the Mediterranean that the destroyers left us, and we carried on alone. I guess the captain was relieved when we finally arrived, for German U-boats were in the habit of lurking in the waters round the Cape, waiting with their torpedoes to pick off any slow-moving cargo ships.

Landfall at the Cape of Good Hope was a wonderful experience. As the mist cleared over Table Mountain, revealing the shining white houses spread up the sloping hills from the sparkling sea, I knew that I had arrived on the continent of my dreams. The long journey by train to the North, through vineyards, across the Karoo Desert and the desolate Kalahari, was full of interest and excitement. At the rear of every carriage was a small open space where you could stand clutching the guard rail of the lurching train, and wiping from your eyes the black smuts of coal which poured from the engine's funnel.

We broke our journey north and stayed all day in Bulawayo, where one of the Southern Rhodesia missionaries took me out to a local hotel for lunch. Here for the first time I came face to face with colonialism. Tables were spread with freshly starched tablecloths, with identical high-backed chairs. Behind each chair was a waiter dressed in brilliant white uniform and wearing spotless white gloves. The waiters moved silently barefoot across the shining jet-black floors, and only their impassive black faces indicated to me that they were not automatons but living individuals.

That evening we changed to another train, and after a full night's journey we crossed the Zambezi into Northern Rhodesia. For one brief moment I caught a glimpse of the smoking wonder of the thundering Victoria Falls and remembered David Livingstone, who eighty-eight years before was the first white man to see them. From there we travelled through an endless forest of trees, stopping every once in a while to fill the engine with water and salute the lonely white ganger. There was nothing to see but trees and more trees, though once we passed an elephant and high in the cloudless sky I saw a great eagle, a black- and white-winged bird which I later came to know as a bateleur.

A minister in Broken Hill

I had been sent by the all-powerful Synod of the church in Northern Rhodesia to take over, for three months, the tiny European congregation of the mining town of Broken Hill, now renamed Kabwe. It was the last thing in the world I wanted to do, for I had not come to Africa to preach to Europeans. I had come to propel Africans into the Kingdom of God. In those days I did not know that my job was not to bring in the Kingdom, but to allow Christ to build it.

They had told me in England that I would be going to Nambala, a mission station out in the bush a hundred miles north from the main town of Lusaka, but the Synod decided otherwise for the moment. Douglas Gray, my boyhood hero and future father-in-law, had suffered from malaria for so long that the Synod had stationed him in this mining town to serve the fifteen or so white families and their children, in his last years before retirement. He was now taking a well-deserved rest in South Africa, so I was asked to take care of his congregation. A little square building with a tin roof had been erected as the church on an odd bit of land down by the shunting yards.

I have few memories of that unhappy time, during which I seemed to wait endlessly for letters from home; but I do remember one occasion when I was invited out, as a matter of courtesy, by the mine manager and his wife to meet one or two other guests. First we gathered for a 'sundowner' at which drinks were served. From somewhere they found an orange juice for Methodist me and then, when everyone was a little merry, we were taken to the spacious dining room of his luxurious house. I had dressed for the occasion in my inappropriately hot black suit and tight clerical collar. I remember nothing of the conversation but was quite astonished to see that between every course—five of them—the guests stretched out their hands to grab a cigarette, leaving me to contemplate the cruet, the silver candlesticks and the lavishly-arranged flowers.

The weekly service in the Methodist chapel was not easy to conduct, because when it rained—and I was there all through the rains—the clatter of a thousand raindrops on the roof drowned out not only my preaching but the organ too. To make matters worse, the railway authorities always seemed to choose a Sunday evening to shunt the wagons of their freight trains in the yards that ran just beside the church windows. What had I, a young man of twenty-four, to say to the rough miners and railway men of this frontier town?

There were a few Catholic missionaries in Broken Hill, but we never met, though sometimes I would slip into their quiet church to pray and watch the nuns silently decorating with flowers the niches of their saints and the demure statue of the Virgin Mary. There was also a very high and rather unsympathetic Anglican priest whose church was not far from mine. After Christmas he wrote me a note, "We Anglicans believe that the hours before Christmas are holy hours of solemnity and repentance. Imagine my consternation when from the Methodist Chapel across the way we heard the noisy sound of carols."

Colonial attitudes

There were three distinct White communities in Broken Hill: the Mine, the Railway, and the Government, and each lived in its appointed place. There were also missionaries, traders and hotel-keepers. There were no poor whites, but hundreds of poor blacks. The black community lived separately in their own townships on the edge of the main European town. I rarely spoke to a black man. Why should I? I had nothing to say to him and he had nothing to say to me.

But I did notice things. Every morning I would see long lines of house and garden 'boys' carrying big blocks of ice from the mine's refrigerator plant to their white masters' houses. At that time there were few domestic refrigerators and a big block of ice would last a day or two, cooling the 'sundowner' drinks or keeping the milk or meat from going off at night. There was also a piece of land outside my house called Toc H Park, through which Europeans might walk, but never an African.

One of the teachers in the morning Sunday school was the wife of an engine-driver called Roy Welensky. I once called on him in his corrugated bungalow down by the shunting yards. By this time he was head of the Railway Workers' Union, and because of the war the Government had made him a nominated member of the colony's Legislative Council. He sat there in his shirt-sleeves, with his copper-coloured arms resting firmly on the coloured oilcloth of his dining table. He had been a boxer in his youth, and he had told his Union that he never went into the ring unless he believed he would win. They would fight the Colonial Government all the way to maintain their high wages and their privileged position as the white gangers, white firemen and white drivers. No black men had ever been trained to do their jobs, so of course the Government gave in. He told me that even though he had left school at an early age, when he spoke in the Legislative Council he never needed notes, because he had successfully studied Pelmanism, a form of memory training.

One day our African minister, the Reverend Joel Njase, took me out to visit a school ten miles away in the bush. He was a wonderful and humorous man who spoke almost incomprehensible English, very fast, with a kind of enthusiastic splutter. We went by bicycle. His was a very old Raleigh Roadster which had no proper 'paddles', only the smooth pedal's centre pin.

I think he was delighted to have a legitimate excuse to escape for a day from his flock's incessant demands for assistance of every kind. He had not only to preach every Sunday in his dilapidated church, baptise their babies, marry them and bury them, but his house was also always full of visitors. They came from his own poverty-stricken home in the Zambezi valley. He was a Tonga by tribe and they were Tonga too, so by African custom he was obliged to offer them his hospitality for as long as they wished to stay with him. As I was later to learn, the family is the bond that holds the African society together. "He is my brother, she is my sister" are the sacred unspoken words which, until the white man came, had been unchallenged.

Teaching at Kafue

In 1944 I was appointed to the Kafue Training Institute, south of Lusaka, to teach Scripture and English, and become the assistant to the Principal. The Kafue Training Institute took boys up to Standard Six, which was the highest academic level at that time available in Northern Rhodesia. Every boy, no matter what his abilities or gifts might be, had to spend time on practical work. This was not just a matter of an hour each day collecting firewood or drawing water, or scuffing the paths, or sweeping the classrooms. Of course they were expected to do all those jobs as a matter of duty; but every boy also took his turn on the building site where we were putting up a house for the women's club, or in the carpenters' shop where they made window and door frames, or on the farm feeding the pigs, or milking the cattle, or in the vegetable garden where they grew cabbages and onions to supplement their staple diet of maize.

I had my own large house, and of course needed to employ a cook/ house boy, called Benny, whose most exciting culinary effort was two poached eggs on spinach. I employed him because he spoke Ci-Ila. In this particular tribe, the Ba-Ila, it is the custom to knock out the six front teeth in the upper jaw. As Benny suffered from constant bouts of asthma and spoke very fast through his non-existent teeth, my language study never got off the ground.[1]

In those days we believed, either consciously or sub-consciously, that Europeans were a superior race, and that we had come from Europe as missionaries to bring a superior culture and a superior religion to an uncultured and heathen people. At Kafue Training Institute we practised a form of cultural apartheid as rigorous as any in the countries that lay to the south of us. The three European families lived in European brick houses protected by mosquito gauze. They kept a local servant boy to cook their food and clean and polish the red cement floors. There was often also a garden boy to chop firewood for the cooking stove and to heat the forty-four-gallon oil drum of bath water. It was a 'them and us' situation. They lived in their small houses and we in our big ones. We never shared food together, nor crossed the threshold of each others' homes. That was how it was and I accepted it. Perhaps there is no better way of describing my life at that time than to quote some passages from my diaries. I have not opened them for over sixty years and they bear the mark of another age, but they reveal how easily I slipped into the missionary culture of that time.

From Merfyn's Kafue Diaries

My work as a teacher

"At nine o'clock I go to the school to teach Standard Six. The scripture lesson developed into a discussion on the true purpose of marriage. We had already discussed polygamy and I tried to emphasise the fact that marriage is not purely physical; also tried to get them to look at it from the woman's point of view. One boy asked me whether sexual intercourse before marriage was a sin. What could I say? It is the usual custom here, especially between cousins and before the girl reaches puberty. Most of the boys

---

1 Merfyn had been sent to Kafue ostensibly to learn Ci-Ila, but the local dialect around Kafue was different to that of Nambala. In addition, the Kafue school students came from many different areas, so English became the common language.

must have had that experience. I could only say that I believed chastity before marriage is the better way; if it is hard for me, God knows it must be hard for them. After that I taught English—the use of idiom; tried to explain the difference between 'hold out', 'hold in', 'hold on', 'hold up'."

"In my Standard Six class is a small boy called Gideon who is the son of the water-drawer and has lived on the mission all his life. He is very intelligent and has managed to get through the early standards of his education in double quick time, with the result that he is about three years younger than the other boys in my class. He is not only intelligent but is also, being a clown, quite disruptive.

"Once when he had tried my patience to the limit I said, "Gideon, I have had enough," then walking down amongst the desks I picked him up bodily—he was a very lean little boy—carried him onto the platform where I was teaching, and plonked him on top of the tall stationery cupboard. He was behind me as I taught, and I was a little surprised to find how often the lids of the desks were being raised by the rest of the class. It was only many years later, when Gideon had become one of my closest friends, that he told me how, from the top of the cupboard, he had made such comic faces that the other boys, exploding with laughter, had been forced to hide their mirth behind their desk lids!

"After tea I played in the staff versus school football match. I think it is good for the Africans to find that they can do something very much better than us Europeans. They certainly ran rings around me on the field today."

Bird-watching

"I played truant from my studies by using my bandaged finger as an excuse for wandering around in the afternoons with field glasses to watch the birds. I had a successful day and spotted a lily trotter, a pied kingfisher and a purple roller. Best of all I spotted the nest of the fish eagles, for which I had been searching for a long time. With the glasses I can see the mother bird on the nest; it is on the opposite bank of the river.

"I was wandering about with the field glasses looking for birds. Suddenly I came across a small native village. I felt very nervous, not knowing the proper etiquette when passing through. I just gave a sheepish *mutende* (universal African greeting) and hurried on. They must have thought me very impolite."

Problems of inequality

"The Principal showed me tonight a letter from one of the teachers, asking for higher wages. He gave his monthly budget and claimed that all his money was spent on food, leaving nothing for amenities. There is constant trouble over wages, and the sense of being unjustly treated rankles so deeply that it completely spoils the relations between African and European. In a nutshell the difficulty is this. The African teachers feel the need to live and work with us, but they naturally compare their standard of living with ours. Here am I in a six-roomed house, with two servants, good clothes, books etc. Alongside me is an African in his three-roomed house, living on mealie-meal porridge, with a wife and family to keep. The gulf is tremendous and although I sometimes feel a twinge of conscience about it, for my African colleagues it is a glaring injustice.

"What is the way of narrowing the gap? Either I must lower my standard of living to his or he must raise his to mine. Taking the first possibility I think that, although by English standards I do not live luxuriously, I could live more simply; but only for ten years or so and only while I am a bachelor. I could cook my own food, but I would lose time which should be spent on other things, and my health would suffer. I could live with fewer books and fewer clothes in a smaller house, but could I do it for long and with a family, without suffering both mentally and physically?

"Now the second possibility: raising the African standard of living. Supposing all of a sudden we gave him the stipend of a European. This would mean four teachers instead of forty and would create a class of men completely out of touch with their fellow Africans. The crux of the matter is this: you cannot raise the standard of living of the teacher alone and leave the rest of the Africans in their poverty. The teacher today compared to our standards is under-nourished and lives in poverty, but compared to the majority of his fellow countrymen he is wealthy."

Thinking about the future

"Nothing matters today but that Audrey is qualified. How good it is to leave my own little cares and shortcomings to rejoice in her triumph! How foolish I was to doubt and waste my heart with anxious thought.

"This evening I have been reading Hort's 'Christian Ecclesia'. It came home very clearly that the disciples were sent out by Jesus 'to preach and to heal'. I am glad Audrey is a doctor because together we will be able to do the real work of an 'apostle'—one who is *sent* to do these two things."

The vegetable garden

Probably because I let it be known that at the age of fourteen I had won the gardening prize at my school, I was given on my arrival at Kafue the responsibility of supervising the growing of vegetables. Down by the river the boys had cleared a patch of ground, and each morning a dozen or so would come for work. The hoeing and the weeding was only a small part of their task, for most of their time was spent lugging water in four-gallon used paraffin tins up the steep bank and pouring it on the dry ground. However hard they worked there never seemed to be enough water, so in an attempt to simplify their job, I made a kind of Egyptian *shaduf*, with a counterweight on the other end of a pole; but it was not a great success.

The river garden

On very hot days, in the late afternoon after school, I would go down to walk beneath the cool trees by the swiftly-flowing water of the Kafue River. We called it our River Garden. It was a garden untouched by human hands and the nearest I have ever known to the Garden of Eden. There was a school of hippos that honked and yawned and spouted noisy jets of water into the evening air.

Downstream was Bulengo, the hill we called 'Livingstone's Hill' because it was here that he realised he could no longer follow the Kafue river, as ahead lay the impenetrable Kafue gorge. Across on the south bank was the steep cliff which sends back a perfect echo of your voice. This is where the baboons live, chattering all the time with other members of the troop and leaping miraculously up the sheer rock face. At the foot of the cliff is a shallow cave to which the people went at times of drought to pray for rain. I never went there myself, for I knew it to be a sacred place for them.

Audrey arrives

I received news that Audrey would be passing through Kafue on her way to Broken Hill to stay with her father. Instead of waiting at Kafue station, I thought I would surprise her by getting on another train going in the opposite direction and board her train as it passed through Mazabuka.

I was to get a shock. In my absurd imagination Audrey had remained unchanged for two years. I can best explain what happened that night by quoting from her own memoirs, written fifty years later.

> At this time Merfyn was stationed at Kafue Mission, which was one hundred and thirty miles south of Broken Hill, so he planned to board my train several stations before that and travel with me to Broken Hill. I had no knowledge of these plans and was astonished when he walked into my compartment on the train.
>
> During my last years in England I had started to smoke very occasionally when relaxing and never dreamt of mentioning this to Merfyn in my letters—it seemed no big deal and it never occurred to me that he would be shocked. He had sometimes smoked a pipe as a student. However he found me on the train reading a novel and smoking a cigarette and was horrified— the whole episode probably illustrating how different I must have seemed to him from the woman he had last seen two years before. Our unshared experiences in that time stretched like a gulf between us. He grabbed my box of cigarettes and threw them out of the window. I said nothing but remember thinking: "That's not going to solve this problem." And in fact it took us both many months to realise how far apart we had drifted and to rediscover each other.

We had doubts and uncertainties almost until our wedding day, but eventually we grew close once more and started our married life chastened and wiser from the experience.

Nambala: Settling In

My first impressions of Nambala

"NAMBALA IS A VERY PRETTY SPOT. It is smaller of course than Kafue, but there is an atmosphere of friendliness which one does not get in the same way at Kafue. I came out here by lorry. Fortunately it was a new one with a good African driver, who spared it over the rough places in the road. I had the front seat, the African passengers just piled up on top of the load outside. We covered the 100 miles in six hours. There were clouds about so it did not get very hot. Naason the cook is looking after me well. Mrs Harrison has a good vegetable garden and keeps hens, so I get plenty of eggs. The house is quite large with a good bath and plenty of hot water when I want it. The garden is full of orange trees and poinsettias." *June 1945*[1]

The orchard and garden

"I find it hard to believe that I have been here a fortnight. I'm still very much in love with life. I killed my first snake last week with my hippo-hide sjambok—a five-foot green tree snake. As I told you, the house is surrounded by a citrus orchard, and just now the trees are laden with oranges. Sorry to tantalise you, but think of going out to pick your own grapefruit for breakfast, and when you are thirsty just popping out to get a tangerine—we call them *naartjis* here. I am beginning to make compost, so that when the rains come, I can have humus for the vegetable garden. I'm determined that Audrey shall not lack for fresh vegetables. I pay a picanin (child) 2d a day to go round collecting old grass and rubbish. I thought I

1 Dates refer to extracts from Merfyn's letters to his parents.

would make him a sledge to help him carry the stuff—wheelbarrows are difficult to get. However like most of my labour-saving devices, it takes two men to do the work of one." *June 1945*

Mumbwa

"Mumbwa, the Government station, is a well-laid-out place. The aerodrome consists of three long grass runways—I thought it was just a very extensive playing field. It is no more than a landing ground for the plane which takes mail from Lusaka to Mongu, away in Barotseland. There is a school, a dispensary, the Boma[2] and of course the District Commissioner's house. This gentleman, one of the old school who came out in 1904, gave me rather a cold reception because he had expected me by plane last Thursday, and I was late for the exams, which he had had to start himself. I felt he was about to ask me any moment which school I had been to, but anyhow he soon thawed and gave me tea and biscuits, my first meal since breakfast.

Nambala mountain

"Chief Mono's village is near Nambala mountain so I decided to climb it. Only one other European has done so in the last ten years. Before I got to the top I understood why! It is what story books call "impenetrable bush" to within 100 feet of the top, then it is as good a rock scramble as anything I did in the Lakes or Wales. What a thrill when I was up. I could see my Circuit—2,000 square miles of it. I could see nearly 60 miles in one direction over the Kafue Flats. Little rock squirrels sat round and chattered at me. I watched a circling eagle from above; I shall go up there again if ever I become depressed." *June 1945*

Learning to speak the language of the people

When I first went to Nambala, I was still too shy to speak Ci-Ila, the local language, so I persuaded Mr Harrison, my Superintendent Minister, to let me go and live in a village. Very reluctantly, he agreed. He arranged for a grass shelter to be built near the house of a retired Evangelist. He loaded his car with a camp bed, chair and table, and having lent me his 'garden boy' as my cook, he equipped him with a kettle and a large iron cooking

---

2 *Boma* is the widespread vernacular term for a stockade, which came to be used for the district government offices.

pot for making bread. Then he took me to a village thirty miles away from the Mission. He muttered something about "these young missionaries wanting to pig it in the bush with the Africans." He and his wife had quickly learned to keep 'the African' in his place.

After three days with the Evangelist walking through the bush politely naming flowers and trees, I knew I was getting nowhere. The next day I got on my bicycle and rode off to a neighbouring village where not a soul spoke English.

I had swotted up one phrase in Ci-Ila: "I have come to your village; please will you help me to speak your language?" They crowded around me, chattering away sixteen to the dozen, and I did not understand a word. But there was one middle-aged lady who seemed to have nothing much to do. She took me in hand, and sitting me on a stool in the shade of one of the huts, she began to teach me. Pointing to the women drawing water from the village well, she said slowly and clearly in the language of the people, "Those women are drawing water from the well." Stumblingly I repeated her words, not once but many times. Then she took two maize cobs, and laying them on the dusty ground she pointed to one and said, 'father', then to the other 'mother'; then she laid down six smaller cobs saying 'children', 'boy', 'girl', 'brother', 'sister'. The days were long and hot, and the stool miserably uncomfortable; but my mentor was indefatigable, her patience inexhaustible. All day long she sat and taught me. She seemed to have neither husband nor children, and I wondered uncharitably whether perhaps she might be the village prostitute. Within two weeks I was preaching in the language of the people.

During those weeks in Chikanka's village, I learned a great deal more than how to stumble through a Ci-Ila sentence. From my stool by the headman's house, I watched the women as they winnowed their kaffir corn[3] and pounded their mealies. At evening time I helped old Chikanka water his cattle. It was arduous work, for the well was deep and the windlass broken. A benevolent Government had sunk the well and provided the windlass, the chain and the bracket; but no-one in the village had bothered to tighten the bolts when they worked loose, or to put any grease on the spindle. After a few months of neglect it broke, and no one cared to mend it, so with aching back and sore hands I pulled up the chain hand over hand.

3 Colloquial term for sorghum, an indigenous grain and still a staple food for much of Africa.

There was a child in the village who lay on a reed mat all day. Her legs and arms were so covered with scabies that she could not move about. There was a man who sat all day making baskets. He had a filthy piece of cloth tied round his head. One day he took it off and I saw that his scalp was a mass of suppurating sores. I asked why he did not go to the hospital in the town. He replied that it was too far to walk, and he had no bicycle nor any money to hire one. There had been a good grain harvest that year, which meant a big surplus for the brewing of beer. Never a night passed but I heard the drums in some village where the people danced and drank all night. So it was that I learnt about the people whom Christ would call to be the living stones from which to build His church.

I made friends with the village blacksmith. He was deaf and dumb, so I was at no greater disadvantage than any other villagers in my conversation with him. This man was to help me in my first efforts to share the gospel in the village. I had learned to use a native adze, with which I carved a six-foot wooden cross which I set up by the well. I went to see the blacksmith and bought an iron spearhead, which he had fashioned out of an old car spring. His anvil was a short length of railway track, and his charcoal fire was blown up with goat-skin bellows, worked by his eight-year-old son.

I hammered the spearhead into the cross and asked a visiting preacher to explain to the mystified villagers that on such a cross had their Saviour been crucified and the spear was man's sin which had been the cause of his death. I planted zinnia seeds at the foot of the cross and some of the women helped to gather thorn bushes to make a fence round the little garden to keep cattle and goats away. I heard later that soon after I left, someone stole the spear, the flowers died from lack of water, and the white ants ate the cross. I had a lot more to learn than the language.

Plans for getting married

"You ask if we are to be married in the Cape. As a matter of fact we just don't know where to get married, but it certainly won't be in South Africa. For some reason this District has no system of leave for men in their first term—they just wait for their health to break down, then send them on sick leave. Unfortunately I have never felt better in my life. We have booked rooms for our honeymoon at a hotel in the Vumba eastern mountains of Southern Rhodesia." *October 1945*

The long-awaited wedding, March 1946

How could I possibly get on with my work with Audrey there in the country and me with little chance to see her? Whenever it became too hard to bear, I developed excuses such as 'toothache' that demanded I should go to Broken Hill to see a dentist. We did manage to meet a number of times, and I became quite an experienced burglar, climbing at night through various of my friends' windows.

At last the time of our wedding arrived, and in the little thatched church on top of Chipembi's hill we were married by Audrey's father. An account of that memorable day is taken from Audrey's memoirs:

At last my contract as a government medical officer was complete and I was free to concentrate on my own affairs once more. I spent a few days in Lusaka with Mrs Nightingale, the Methodist Chairman's wife, shopping for her, making my own wedding dress and Margaret's bridesmaid's frock, buying a going-away outfit and collecting accessories. I arranged the flowers and the cake, both gifts from two of the long-standing farming families in the Chipembi area who had known me as a child. I returned to my family in Broken Hill and finally we all set out with Merfyn and the wedding cake, in an open truck to Chipembi. Kenneth Johnson, the missionary in charge and Merfyn's great friend, was best man, Margaret my sister was bridesmaid and my father conducted the service. There was a feast afterwards seated round the kitchen table at the farm and many of the guests were from the surrounding farms who remembered me from my childhood days.

Thirty years before this, Audrey's father Douglas Gray had been given a vision, granted to no other missionary of that time. Starting with twelve girls, he would establish a school to provide an education for girls, in every way equivalent to that being given to boys. His vision came true, and he built a school for 150 girls drawn from every corner of Zambia. Now here was his daughter fully trained as a doctor, marrying the son of his greatest friend at college. No wonder he was overcome with emotion. I was aware of him stopping now and again during the service to take control of his quivering lips and shaking voice. However, no-one had thought to invite the girls in the school, whose chapel we were using, to the wedding. A year later the girls said to me *"Muluti* (Reverend), why were we not invited? Maneli Gray, your father-in-law, is our father also, and to see his daughter married would have been a time of great joy for us." Somehow these words were a rebuke that still brings shame to me.

Audrey at Nambala

When I first arrived at Nambala, I had come to replace one of the District's two black ministers. One of these, the Rev. James Mulala with his wife Bessie and their three children, moved to the adjoining circuit of Keembe, which had no minister at all, white or black. Keembe was an area which Douglas Gray had himself pioneered during the 1920s and 1930s. There were no church buildings in these circuits, but there were several primary schools strung out over a distance of about a hundred miles. Each school, built by the villagers themselves, had a trained headmaster and his assistant, offering a four-year basic education for 7-11 year olds. Most of the children were boys, because mothers needed their daughters at home to help with everything, from drawing water and pounding the maize, to gardening and caring for younger children.

With James Mulala's removal to the adjoining circuit, his house at Nambala became available for Audrey and me to occupy, but of course it had to be brought up to 'European' standards. My superintendent ordered from South Africa a very light balsa-like wood to make new ceilings in the lounge, dining room and bedroom. The verandas were netted with permanent mosquito gauze and a brick kitchen was built outside the back door. Two forty-four-gallon petrol drums were mounted on burnt brick behind the bathroom. Our wood-chopping garden boy would light a roaring fire at three o'clock every day under the lower of the two tanks. As the water heated it would move to the top tank. Unfortunately someone had forgotten to order a bath, but Jack Merry, our resident prospector, came to our rescue. He kept pigs to make his own bacon, but it was off-season for pigs so he lent us the tin bath in which he usually made up the brine to cure the bacon. Everything was fine until Audrey invited her sister Margaret to come and spend part of their honeymoon with us at Nambala. I built a grass shelter for them in the garden, and slapped a coat of white paint on our rather dingy-looking bath. On the first night her husband Tom stuck firmly to the paint. We prised him out and used a white cotton sheet to line the bath for future occasions.

I have never rightly understood how Audrey managed that first year of our marriage. Within a month she was ill with regular morning sickness, but still she cycled down to the dispensary every day, desperately trying to pick up some snatches of conversation from our medical orderly. Her vocabulary was almost entirely medical—cough, cold, malaria, syphilis, hernia, malnutrition etc. On one occasion a nine-year-old girl was wheeled in by her father on his dilapidated bicycle. She was terribly thin and quite unable to walk. Audrey immediately recognised the child's disease: it was rickets and she knew just what to prescribe. Three months later the girl was working alongside her mother in the homestead garden and Audrey's reputation had shot through the roof. She had become a very special kind of witch doctor.

It must seem almost impossible for people these days to realise just how cut off we were. Our letters arrived on the passenger truck which ran once a week between Lusaka and Mumbwa. One of our workmen would borrow the Mission bicycle, pedalling the ten miles through heat and rain to the Boma at Mumbwa to collect our mail.

Trials of the missionary wife

During the first years of our marriage, one major problem stood between us. It was a problem that Mary Livingstone had experienced with her husband David. Audrey did not like Dr Livingstone; I think indeed she hated him, because he kept going off on his travels leaving his wife behind to look after the children. Perhaps she had the same feelings about her own father, and now here she was, landed with a husband who was doing the same thing all over again.

In hindsight I can try to imagine what it must have been like for Audrey, a woman all on her own with her nearest white neighbours ten miles away at Mumbwa, where the only means of contact was to send some-one off on the mail bike to ask for help. Once during the dry season, a bush fire leapt over the 'fire guard', the ten-yard strip of slashed grass that surrounded the mission station. Leaving the children to manage on their own, she leapt on her bicycle, and riding through the blinding smoke, rushed off to summon help from Sam Luwisha, our right-hand man. For-tunately the wind dropped and the house did not burn down.

Once when she was feeding Robin in the bedroom she heard Mary Jane's terrified screams coming from the mulberry trees that surrounded the house. Putting Robin on the floor she ran outside to see Mary Jane standing face to face with a spitting cobra which had reared its swaying body from the grass. Mary Jane was only three feet tall herself.

Snakes were always a problem. It was all right if they came during the day because the cook could handle them, but it was a different story at night, when the smaller ones got into the house slithering along our polished floors. Audrey had seen me dispatch them using the flat head of the house broom, so she had learned to do the same. Spiders were another thing, not the little ones but the tarantulas. A broom was no good for them because they ran too fast, but if you could corner them, then a kettle of boiling water poured over them would do the trick.

For me of course it did not seem a big problem, for in a missionary's life the only thing that matters is 'the work'. If that meant going away to visit the schools in the Keembe circuit, Audrey would have to 'trust in the Lord and keep her powder dry', in the words of Cromwell. But for a woman all on her own, that is easier said than done.

Nambala: Home and Family

IN SIX YEARS FROM 1946 we had four children—Ruth, Mary Jane, Robin and Patricia—and between pregnancies Audrey continued to work her magic in the dispensary. I was meanwhile very busy doing all the things which seemed at the time to be so vitally significant for the building of the Kingdom of God on African soil. The only time we had together was when the sun went down over the Nambala hills. Sometimes I would wind up our portable gramophone and we would hear over and over again Dvořák's New World symphony, but most of the time we read novels by authors such as Charles Morgan, Nevile Shute and H.E.Bates.

Merfyn and Audrey's house at Nambala. The brick kitchen was added at left

Our first child, Ruth—December 1946

The nearest hospital was 100 miles away in Lusaka so, when the time drew near for our first baby to be born, I had to send Audrey to stay for a fortnight or so with friends in town.[1] One day a group of government officers arrived at the Boma for consultation with the District Commissioner and I was invited to meet them for a 'sundowner'. One of them said "I heard from a nurse in the European hospital that you have a new baby."

"Is that so?" I said, and dashed back to Nambala to collect enough petrol for the journey into town. As I was pumping the petrol from our 44-gallon drum, a message came from Mono, our local Chief, saying that his wife was having trouble giving birth to her first child. Please would I take her with me in the back of the vanette? "But of course," I said, not realising that it was not only the Chief's wife I had offered to take, but her own mother, her mother-in-law, and an unspecified number of women relatives.

It was raining cats and dogs, and the gravel on the road, which had recently been repaired by prisoners from the jail, was a sea of mud. After a couple of hours of slipping and sliding from one side of the road to the other, my overloaded vanette finally sank down to its springs in the gooey mud. I had an axe in the car and the Chief's wife's relatives cut down branches from the trees by the roadside. They stuffed these valiantly beneath the spinning wheels, but to no avail.

Three hours later, as the sun filtered through the heavy cloud, some villagers arrived but soon saw that nothing could be done. Without a word they disappeared into the bush again, muttering the word *ngombe, ngombe* (cattle). Half an hour later they appeared with four yoked oxen and a hooked chain. They dragged me onto firm ground. I put my foot down on the accelerator, and going like the wind, went straight to the African hospital. They told me later that the Chief's wife had delivered twins. What would I have done had they arrived when I was stuck in the mud?

When I arrived at the European hospital, there was Audrey wreathed in smiles with our daughter Ruth in her arms. Such rejoicing!

"Oh my! Oh my! What a day! What a day!" said Mr Mole, as he stood at the door of his burrow that beautiful summer's morning.[2]

---

1 Each subsequent delivery involved a similar family exodus: Audrey to Lusaka to await the latest, while the children went to stay at Kafue with Merfyn's brother David, who now headed up the Kafue Teacher Training Institute.

2 *Wind in the Willows*

Preparing for the Retreat

"It is eight o'clock in the evening and we are in bed. No it is not malaria—just that we have had the painters in today and everything is all upside down, so after supper we thought the best place was bed. Such cleanings and polishing as never were seen before. Audrey is determined to have the house neat and clean for the Retreat next Monday. Unfortunately only men are coming so I don't suppose anyone will notice that the brass has an added lustre and the table legs as well as the top have been polished. In the garden I am getting all the mulberry trees pruned and I have a gang of boys working frantically to get the new garage completed in time to house the Chairman's car. Sam Luwisha who usually supervises the work outside is on a month's leave so I have to watch the men—Flower,

Ruth carried in a cut-out kerosene tin: South Africa, 1947

Tie and Wankie who are cementing the hospital outhouse, Shamazongo and Ian who are whitewashing, Thomas and Ngulube who are cutting poles for the new cattle kraal. I also have a gang of picanins doing odd jobs about the place; I pay them in oranges—12 for two-and-a-half hours' work." *July 1948*

Our new house

"The rains have begun in earnest—we had four-and-a-half inches one night. I'm very glad that at last the roof of the new house is on. We are working hard to be in by Christmas, but plastering, putting up ceilings and fitting doors and windows take a long time. We are in a wonderful pickle just now because we have reached the stage when the end wall of the old house has to be knocked out to join us up with the new wing." *December 1948*

Our second child, Mary Jane—June 1949

Audrey, now pregnant with our second child, had to go into Lusaka town to be near the hospital. The District Officer and his wife, now living in Lusaka, have offered to put us up. They live in one of the 'pre-fab' houses put up during the war for Government staff. Made from local material, they have thatched roofs, fatal for my asthma, so I was in hospital too. However all went well for Audrey, and a second bonny baby was born. We could not think of a name, so we just called her Mary Jane.

A companion on my rounds

"Ruth is settling down with her new nanny, Rosy. She sometimes comes with me when we go on our rounds to see the pigs, the garden and the building operations. She insists on calling mealies 'meliums' and takes her doll with her everywhere. We have put the carpet down in the nursery and it is a delight, especially this cold weather." *June 1950*

Getting some respite in the town

"Here we are in Broken Hill. I am going off tomorrow for a tour in the Bulenje and leaving Audrey and the children here for the week. Audrey is not having too good a time—it's not just morning sickness, it is twenty-four hours a day sickness and I could not leave her on her own at Nambala. I was very glad of a comfortable car to bring her in here. We had Mary Jane on the front seat, while Ruth travelled behind with the cook, the baggage and the cat with her six kittens. Setting out on a journey is a major operation when you have to pack everything from food to soap and boot polish for a week in the bush." *August 1950*

Snakes and spiders in the house

"The weather is really beginning to get warm and any work between 11 and 4 is tiring in the extreme. It is cooler in the evenings but the pressure lamps make the rooms very hot. This is the season for snakes. We have killed three round the house in the last few days. I caught a huge spider the other day and showed it to our Game Ranger who is something of a naturalist. He thinks it may be a new species and has sent it to the Bulawayo Museum for identification." *September 1950*

Visitors to the station

"Hardly a day passes but we get visitors. I mean apart from the stream of Africans who pass through. Today it was one of the Indian Moslem traders whose child was sick and he wanted Audrey's advice. He brought a gift of pineapples and other fruit which was very welcome. Yesterday it was a Lithuanian farmer out to get labour, whose car broke down and he came in for help. The day before that Bill Bullock called in on his way out to round up some stray elephants, and also the Agricultural Officer who wanted to buy some of our oranges." *September 1950*

The vagaries of housekeeping

"We had a perfect example this week of the vagaries of housekeeping. We got up on Saturday morning and Audrey remarked that we should have to open a tin of bully beef for lunch, as there was nothing else in the house. In the night however a wild cat had got into the chicken house and bitten the heads off two chickens, so we had them stewed. Then a boy arrived from the Kafue River with fresh bream; the mail boy came back from the Boma with 4lbs of beef—an ox had been killed; and at tea time the Game Ranger turned up with a leg of kudu. How can one plan a menu?" *November 1950*

Christmas fun

"We had a hectic time before Christmas with parcels arriving and secret preparations going on after Ruth had gone to sleep. The little tea service arrived—Ruth is going to get a great deal of fun out of it. I was busy making dolls' coat hangers in odd moments for the dolls' wardrobe, and doing a lot of painting of old toys to make them new for Christmas. But all was ready by first light on Christmas day when the children came into our bedroom. First the stockings had to be emptied and enthused over to the last sweet and monkey nut. Then Ruth uncovered the newly-painted dolls' beds, each with its newly-dressed doll. How Mary Jane hugged hers! Up to now she has had to make do with Ruth's when she wasn't watching. Last of all came the dolls' wardrobe, red with white ducks painted on the drawers; inside on little hangers were the new dresses Audrey had made and the old ones dyed and trimmed." *December 1950*

Scouting

"This week I have been a Boy Scout. I have been running a camp on our 'estate'. Last night we had a big camp fire when most of the Europeans from the Boma came over. The game ranger had shot a sable antelope which he gave us for our camp fire. We hung juicy steaks over the flames, just the way the South African Boers do. Never have I tasted better meat. We raised £10 for our district Scout Fund and it was a very happy occasion. At several points in the programme, we put on little sketches, but I find the sketch of 'Oscar the Jumping Flea' to be quite lost on the African. Far more effective has been when I have stuffed a pillow under my shirt and appear as a very corpulent pugilist. I challenge the smallest Scout in the troop to a bout of fisticuffs and the spectators' delight is unbounded as I am repeatedly knocked down by him.

"I played in goal last Saturday in a football match and let four goals through. After the game our opponents marched round the field, as the victors always do, and the song of triumph consisted of a very simple refrain: 'We sing in praise of Tempulu, Tempulu, for his glorious work for us this afternoon.'" *December 1950*

Shopping in Lusaka

"I am back home again after three days in Lusaka where I was glad to find Audrey looking very well and having a restful time with Mr. and Mrs. Shaw while she waits for the baby [Robin]. Then a day at Kafue where I could hardly recognise Ruth and Mary Jane, they had grown so much. Mary Jane is the winsomest child I have ever met. Of course they are having the time of their lives with their cousins Richard and Elizabeth and the other children there. I think we shall have to make a practice of frequent visits between Nambala and Kafue.

"One of my vivid memories of missionary life will be the hectic days of shopping whenever I go into the Line of Rail.[3] I come back with the car absolutely loaded to capacity, carrying for example 100 lbs. of sugar, 100 lbs. of flour, a duster for James Mulala to clean the Keembe communion plate, six footballs for the village schools, a sewing machine for the medical orderly's wife, a month's order of groceries in tins and bottles, engine oil, engine parts for the pump and maize-grinding machine, materials for

---

3 Most of the industry and population of Zambia is concentrated in the area known as the Line of Rail, along the railway that links the Copperbelt with Lusaka and Livingstone.

the children's dresses and wool, a 'saucepan wireless set' so I can listen in for news of the new baby's arrival, fifty empty sacks for the villagers' contribution of maize to the District Extension Fund, a parcel of books for sale in the Nambala cooperative store, bibles, catechisms, books on farming and carpentry, medicines for the dispensary, a new pair of shorts and vegetable seed for the garden." *February 1951*

Our third child, Robin—March 1951

"As we have no telephone, I had arranged with the Director of Broadcasting to send me the announcement of my child's birth over the radio, in the Ci-Tonga programme. When it came, I did not know whether the word they used was for a boy or a girl! I rushed outside to find an African who could tell me. "It's a boy, it's a boy," he said. I think it is probably a good thing to have daughters first—it gives the parents a chance to get some practice with docile girls before obstreperous boys come along. I hope you like the name Robin Gray. If he grows up to combine the great-hearted grace of my father John Robinson Temple with the pioneer spirit of Audrey's father, Sidney Douglas Gray, he will be some man!" *March 1951*

A new pantry for Audrey

"I have made a dream pantry for Audrey, all painted in pale green. There are hooks, shelves, drawers and a linoleum-covered worktop, and there are labelled tins—for everything from breadcrumbs to nutmeg. It is a great secret till Audrey comes home to see it for herself." *April 1951*

Luxury of a refrigerator

"We brought back with us a paraffin fridge, the first we have ever had ourselves. A consignment had just come in, so I took the plunge and spent all the money (£50) I have been putting aside for a new car. It was great fun unpacking it from its crate and getting it to work. Paraffin lamps are always a bit tricky. Today we made ice-cream. Mary Jane shovelled it in till her cheeks bulged, and then when her mouth was absolutely full she chewed it. It is going to be a real boon, especially when the hot weather comes in October.

"Ruth is getting quite keen on her alphabet picture books and is quite good at distinguishing letters. Mary Jane is a most adorable and very naughty child, and is terribly difficult to be cross with. Sometimes she

Mary Jane, Audrey, and Ruth, 1949

cries at night asking to come into our room. We threaten, cajole, shut the door, put her to sleep in the study, then just when we think that the battle is won she comes padding down the passage, all dressed up in her dressing gown and slippers and before we can say 'knife' she has climbed into our bed. I am afraid she is going to break many hearts before she is done. Robin is still too much of a baby to have impinged on my consciousness yet."*May 1951*

Fire and frost

"Another veldt fire swept down on us last week. We frantically tried to burn the grass back to meet it, but suddenly the wind changed, threatening our own home. In the end we only lost three kitchens, which were burnt to the ground, and two grain bins for the mission: all of which makes life very much worth living, but is not conducive to getting the Prayer Letter finished. I wish we could say we had lots of parsley and spinach in the garden; however in one night the frost killed all our tomatoes, egg-plants and beans. Now there is no water and we have no vegetables at all; poor Audrey no sooner gets one item of our menu under control, than some other source of supply dries up." *June 1951*

Entertaining the children

"We shall be glad when the cold weather is over, as the cold before breakfast seems to make the children very weepy and whiny. While Audrey is feeding Robin, I take them out to feed the baby chicks. How Ruth and Mary Jane love mixing the mash with hot water. They now play very well together inventing all sorts of games. One evening Ruth, well suppered, bathed and in her night-dress, put Mary Jane to bed all by herself. This is a great help to Audrey and myself." *July 1951*

The Christmas parcel

"Thank you for the last registered letter for Ruth with cut-outs and multi-coloured ribbons. The children love getting things and 'Grandma in England' remains a very real person to Ruth. When the mail came saying you had sent off a Christmas parcel, we told the children. That evening when we were sitting reading, Mary Jane appeared in the doorway; we scolded her back to bed but she burst into tears and said she had only wanted to come and get her 'Christmas'. She is a very sweet child and it seems a pity she will have to grow up, but is still naughty about her meals; she just goes on strike and pushes her plate away." *September 1951*

Enforced household management

"I had to entertain Laycock, my scouting friend, single-handed the whole day, plus look after the children, as Audrey was two days in bed with a temperature—flu or fever. No Grandma or maiden aunt to call on out here, so I seemed to spend the time sieving spinach, emptying pots and trying to keep the children out of the 'lovely mud' in the yard. Running a circuit is child's play, compared to running a family. Hence the vital importance of books and letters from you and papers too, although I do wonder what I would do without the children. They provide constant entertainment. Mary Jane is the most amusing little person. Ruth rushed in from the walk with her 'nurse girl' Janet today and dragged me into the house and sat me down because she said she had a 'very big sort of kind of story to tell me'—of course it was nothing very much, but she was full of it." *November 1951*

Our friends at the Boma

"At Mumbwa, the Government station ten miles away, there is a little group of Europeans, mostly Government officials, whom I meet on the Development team. The District Commissioner, son of a Scottish manse; the Agricultural Officer, whose father was an Irish minister; the Water Development Engineer; the Policeman; a District Officer from New Zealand; a building contractor and their wives and families. They all attend service with our African members on special occasions and they are our very good friends. They are easy to mix with in their work, at their tennis parties and their sundowners; but I long to give them the salt that alone can give savour to their apparently jolly, but in fact rather dreary lives. Will you pray that I may be able to help them at the deep level where their need is as great as the Africans amongst whom they are working. Good race relations are made, not by Conference pronouncements, but by the respect that each community learns to have for the other." *Prayer Letter 6: May 1952*[4]

Our fourth child, Patricia—October 1952

"You will have had the wire by now giving news of another grand-daughter. She is very like Ruth was when she was born, though with not such a round face. We have had great difficulty in choosing a name for her. I wanted to call her Cherry, but that found no favour so I think she will be Patricia Margaret." *October 1952*

Bringing the family home

"I feel like a cat with kittens. Last week I brought home Audrey and the two youngest from Broken Hill, and I leave at 3am tomorrow to fetch Ruth and Mary Jane from Kafue. It was David's idea, and it has enabled Audrey to settle down here and get the two babies into a routine before the

---

4 Merfyn wrote eleven Prayer Letters in his second tour at Nambala, the first in May 1950 as he returned by ship to Africa and the last in January 1955, six weeks before he "sailed for home." In the first letter he explains why he is writing them:

"I came to feel with increasing conviction as I went round on deputation that a new approach must be made to strengthen the bands that bind us in the Younger Churches to you at home … As many of you know the burden of my message on deputation has been that benevolent interest in the Mission is not enough; our urgent need today is for those who will give themselves in prayer … My hope is that through a regular correspondence with you I can present the needs of our people in N. Rhodesia in such a way as shall make it possible for you to pray for specific people & actual problems that face us in our work."

two girls arrive. How excited the girls will be to be home again, though I expect they will be sorry to say goodbye to their cousins.

"Patricia is a good baby; she doesn't keep us awake at nights and sleeps most of the day. It is taking time for Robin to get adjusted. He objects vigorously if I try to bath him or feed him or put him to bed; he has obviously grown up to prefer a woman's gentler touch. Robin is going to be a mechanic as he has a passion for tools and nuts and bolts. He can't see a wheelbarrow or cart or a pram without asking to get under it to mend it." *November 1952*

A church in Mumbwa

"I had a meeting yesterday at Mumbwa with some of the Europeans who are getting quite keen on the idea of building a church there. We want to build a church for both Europeans and Africans together, and the District Commissioner and some of the others are keen to start right away digging the foundations themselves and bricklaying. It will cause quite a sensation to see Europeans and Africans working together with picks and shovels." *November 1952*

Christmas parties for all

"We had a children's party at the Boma on Christmas Eve—a big Christmas tree and lots of little presents for the children from the Boma folk. On Christmas Day we started of course with the stockings, then the Christmas service here, 150 Africans and 20 Euro-

peans in our little church. What a service it was! Never again. We tried to mix the dignity of a church service with a congregation from the villages—howling babies and people rolling up any old time. It is all very well to say that we will have no colour bar in the church; our difficulty is not the difference in colour, but the difference of culture and language and tradition.

"Then we had tea and mince pies and Christmas cake under the shade of the big fig tree. I think the Europeans were glad to get away from the Boma for a while. Fortunately we had forgotten to prepare a Christmas dinner because the children were far too excited to eat. At 12.30 we sat down to bread and cheese and bananas.

"Then at 4 o'clock we had a party for the African children, who live on the Mission. They came—15 of them—and sat solemnly eating bread and jam on the veranda, drinking pink synthetic raspberry juice, and finishing with mangoes and sweets. Then they played on our children's swings and pushed round the dolls' prams and gave each other rides in Robin's push-cart. Malumba's two eldest girls took Patricia for a walk in her pram—such shrieks of delight and scampering about as you never did see—they didn't leave until 7 pm. Ever since the children have been as cross as can be; I wish we could have Christmas by instalments." *January 1953*

The children are growing up

"I wonder if Robin reminds you of me when I was two? His interests are very masculine. When I arrived home this morning from my appointment at Mono village, I found Mary Jane busily washing her dolls' frocks and Robin under the car with a spanner. His hands are into everything, and nothing is safe unless it's put away on top of the wardrobe or locked up. Patricia is very much like Mary Jane was at this age; we often wish you could share our joy in her because we remember how you loved Mary Jane as a baby. Audrey thinks she is more precocious than the others—she now claps her hands when requested to do so. I think she is more spoilt than the others ever were." *July 1953*

White mice join the family

"Ruth of course is now home from Kafue[5], and although Audrey is going to make the attempt, it is by no means easy to make time for lessons when Patricia, Mary Jane and Robin are so very demanding. Last week I got four white mice for the children—Robin has since let one escape. We keep them in the garden in a paraffin box with a glass side. Audrey tolerates them because she thinks it helps the children to understand the 'facts of

---

5 Ruth was going to school at Kafue, some 150 miles from Nambala, where she lived with Merfyn's brother David. This arrangement however did not last, as David soon left Kafue and Ruth spent another brief time at school on the Copperbelt—see below.

life'. Mary Jane lets them crawl all over her. I enjoy making rope ladders for them out of string and paperclips." *April 1954*

Goats are a mixed blessing

"Our two Swiss goats arrived in Lusaka and two days later they were brought here in a Land-Rover trailer. They are very tame and the children took to them at once, but it will be a long time until we get any milk from them. Then we had a great tragedy today. Ruth went to let the goats out this morning and found that Nancy, Mary Jane's little white ewe, had died in the night. She was in kid too but the cause of death is unknown. Audrey is not fond of the remaining goat. It somehow gets into the house through the back door. It pinched a whole loaf of freshly baked bread off the dining room table and peed copiously on our new sitting room carpet. My attempt to get a fresh milk supply seems doomed to failure. However Polly the brown cow had another calf this week—her last died of foot and mouth in January." *June 1954*

Decisions about the children's school

"I have spent a whole week on the Copperbelt, settling Ruth in with Mr. and Mrs Gray so that she can go to school. She found the first few days rather hard going—everything so strange and new, and when evening came she was very homesick, but I left her yesterday smiling bravely as she waved goodbye. Being a parent I find almost as gruelling as first falling in love.

"We have realised recently that sooner or later we shall have to face up to the problem of educating the children. Ruth's going away has made us sit up and think. To teach them at home is not satisfactory, but we do not want to send them away when they are very young. Ruth's sojourn at Kafue with David's family was an ideal arrangement, but it could only be temporary. It looks as if we shall not be able to come back to a station in the bush, so we must face the prospect of living in town where the children can attend day school. We are not worrying too much, because a way seems to be opening, but we are trying to get used to the idea that we shall not always live the free and easy life of the 'Bush'." *January 1954*

6 Nambala: Evangelism and Ministry

"HERE ARE SOME OF THE FACTORS that dominate the missionary situation in Northern Rhodesia at present:[1]

The people are primitive
By that I mean that they have no civilisation of their own. They are a people with no knowledge of their own past apart from a few oral traditions preserved by the old men. They had no written language until our pioneer missionaries at the turn of the century provided one. Even today the only books published in Ci-Ila, apart from a few school readers, are the New Testament, a hymn book and Pilgrim's Progress. If you can imagine your own life with no knowledge of history beyond a few stories told you by your grandfather, you will begin to understand some of our difficulties – for instance when we set out to explain why there is a difference between the New Testament and the Old.

The people are poor
They live in small villages of mud huts scattered across the veldt. Some of them keep cattle, but large areas are infested with tsetse fly and there no cattle can be kept. They cultivate the land with the hand hoe and when the soil near the village is exhausted they move on to another site. By Western standards their basic needs are easily satisfied. Their staple diet is maize or kaffir corn which is fairly easy to grow; they need few clothes—a couple of shirts and a pair of shorts will last a man for a twelvemonth. They can

---

1 Merfyn's attitudes are quite confronting by the standards of 2010, but they reflect his inexperience, and no doubt the views of his missionary and colonial circle. It is interesting to compare them with the remarks of Chapter 19. See also Editorial Foreword.

build a hut to last them four years within a month. The impermanency of most of the villages makes it impossible to build permanent churches. Our schools are semi-permanent buildings sited in the centre of an inhabited area, and many of the children are weekly boarders, i.e. they come with their food for a week and return home at the weekend to get more food from their parents. The only way for a man to earn money is for him to sell his surplus maize—an industrious man might earn £10 a year in this way—or go to the mines to find work there. A few are employed in the area on the roads or doing other Government work.

Tribal life is fast disintegrating
Under the impact of Western civilisation and modern industry the old social organisation of the African has crumbled. New incentives in the form of wages have broken down the cohesion of the tribe. Their religion, which was part and parcel of the social set-up, has lost its hold, and people are living in a kind of spiritual vacuum. We believe that in Christianity we have the pattern for a new community in Africa." *Prayer Letter 1: May 1950*

My struggles with the language

"I learnt off a little speech in Ci-Ila to answer my welcome in the Quarterly Meeting. It was greeted with enthusiasm; I wonder if they realised how much the three sentences I spoke had cost me? On Friday I heard that Chief Cipansh was holding his court at Mono, three miles away. I decided to go and listen and swotted up a sentence of explanation before going. When I arrived I found that a funeral was in progress and the court had been postponed. My sentence was useless—I tried to say 'Who has died?' but by a mistake with the pronouns, announced to the chief 'You are dead.' I think he was a little surprised, but he was very nice about it." *June 1945*

Living off the land

At first, when travelling, I took a few men with me, to carry my food box, my sleeping bag and my canvas water bottle; and of course I took my cook, complete with iron cooking-pot for making daily bread. But there was the problem of providing food for my carriers, which involved bargaining with the villagers, who knew all too well that the chips were on their side. I was a rich white man and gullible too.

For his village ministry, Merfyn started off by using teams of porters, but the system did not work well and he switched to 'travelling light'

So I took a chance and decided to live off the land, taking only my sleeping bag, canvas water-bottle, tea bags and some small tins of condensed milk. This made all the difference because, instead of the villagers depending on my arrogant self-sufficiency, I became dependent on them.

This was tested out once, when I got lost at night. Through the trees I saw a fire burning, and getting off my bicycle, I began to walk towards the light. Sitting around the fire on stools and large smooth logs were a group of men, women and children. I was alone with no carriers or companion. They saw me dejected, tired and no doubt very hungry. After the usual greetings I saw two men in anxious conversation. They had food, millet meal, but no 'relish'—the groundnuts, meat or fish which add protein to the unappetising carbohydrate meal. One man got on his bicycle and disappeared into the bush. Some time later he returned carrying a chunk of wart hog which I guess had been hanging too long in the trees. I could have done without that, but courtesy demanded that I eat all that was laid before me.

These were ba-Chewa, a very poor people who live in small villages in small houses. With great courtesy the old head-man had swept his own house clean for me. I was his guest. He suggested that I take the bicycle inside the house with me, even though there was hardly room to spread my sleeping bag. I explained that I would have to leave very early, for the distance from his village near Kaoma to Kasempa was not inconsiderable. I would need to travel sixty miles on a little-used path where there are no other villages. At first light there was tapping on my reed door and there was a young girl carrying a basin of warm water. She spoke a little English and explained to me that when she grew up she wanted "to be a doctor to help my people." I wished her well but doubted that a child from this remote village would ever find fees for her secondary school. I wondered whether rumours of Nambala's Dr Audrey Tempulu had spread as far as this, but I never heard what happened to her.

My experiment with a motorcycle

I purchased an ex-army Triumph motorcycle from Mr Dodia, a friendly Muslim trader in Mumbwa. He sold it to me for £30 and taught me how to use it. I called my new bike Boanerges—son of thunder; Africans called it *inchinga ya mulilo* (bicycle of fire). The next week I set off to visit the furthest school in the Keembe circuit, expecting to accomplish the journey in half the time it would take on a bicycle. All went well until I came to the area known as the 'grain bins of the elephants'. Here the grass has canes as thick as your little finger, growing nine feet tall. The track across the plain is very narrow indeed, just the width of a man's shoulders.

The gears on my motorcycle were on the handlebars, and any grass cane which the morning dew had caused to bend across the path would snatch at the lever and put it out of gear. My 'bicycle of fire' was not a success. I have begun to learn that in Africa, speed of travel is not as important as time to talk to others along your path. Once I stopped and asked a traveller how long it might take to reach the next village. "I do not know," he said, "It all depends on who you meet along the way."

Calling the people to repentance

"I came back yesterday from a preaching tour of the villages in the west. I made myself unpopular with my companions by insisting on carrying my own pack; they nearly refused to come with me—said that they would be laughed at if they allowed a white man to carry his own blankets. However I was determined not to be regarded as a D.C. (District Commissioner) or E.O. (Extension Officer). I haven't dared to tell Audrey yet, but I left my food box and lived off the country: eggs, sweet potatoes, pumpkin and mealie-meal. I did carry salt, sugar, tea, dried milk—adequate if not always appetising.

"It is difficult to describe in cold blood our experience on the journey. As we preached and saw men and women repent, the world of the Bible was normal; no claims seemed extravagant, angels and the powers of darkness were no longer just quaint images. Beer-pots were smashed and drunkards converted. One becomes so schooled in caution these days that we dare not claim too much, but in 20 villages 85 people swore to give up their drinking and all the things that follow in the train of the beer pots. It is a big challenge to us—a responsibility that only seems bearable when I am on my knees—but what makes me glad is that we are in touch with the people, not just the educated aristocracy. We can say no more than that God has wrought this thing and it is marvellous in our eyes."
August 1948

Kindled in Some Hearts it is[2]

The pioneer missionaries had not worked long amongst the ba-Ila before they realised that their work was not only evangelism, but a many-sided task of nurture and education. William Chapman, who was the first to pitch his tent under the muchenje tree at Nambala in 1903, said in his book A Pathfinder in South Central Africa, "If a missionary attended only to their spiritual needs, what kind of man would he produce? If instructed in spiritual things only, would they be fitted for the work of life? What sort of Christian character would such training produce? They would be monstrosities not men. Such religious teaching is not enough. Christianity must not be divorced from life but must pervade the whole of man's activities." In Northern Rhodesia we have been set a twofold task; it would be wrong of us to say that one side of it is more important than the other, they are complementary. As revolutionaries we must both transform African rural society so that it becomes the good soil in which the Church takes root and grow healthily bearing much fruit, and we must also plant the seed of a Church that will be a living fellowship under the authority of Christ.

2 From an article written for *The Widening Way: Northern Rhodesian Sketches,* ed. E.G. Nightingale, Cargate Press, 1952

We choose one month in the year, usually August, when we gather a group of Christians from the villages at the mission station for a Bible school. For ten days we sing, pray and search the Scriptures; then we go out together to preach. Our practice is to hold a firelight service in a village in the evening, sleep there overnight, and gather the people again in the morning to make sure that the message of the night before has been driven home. When we have gathered more than eight or ten converts in one village, we form them into a band and ask them to choose their own leader, who generally turns out to be the only literate member amongst them.

I recall one such expedition. Our rendezvous was Chief Chibuluma's village. Coming in from the north, ours was the first column to arrive. We did not look much like soldiers as we marshalled our little band in a clearing outside the village. Perhaps the most military-looking was our leader, the Rev. James Mulala in khaki uniform, old army braces and a peaked toupee. Peter Likanke looked like any other wayfarer, except that he walked barefoot and carried his precious askari boots tied by their laces around his neck. It is true I was wearing an olive green shirt, but no one would know the meaning of the letters USN (United States Navy) on the pocket. My rope-soled shoes were ex-tank corps and my aluminium water bottle bore the mystic letters ARP (Air Raid Precaution).

We sang lustily as we marched in Indian file down the narrow bush path leading to the village. Later that day, the sometimes 'mobile' columns—for African bicycles often seem to be as much pushed as ridden—came in from the South and the West. That evening was the high spot of our campaign. As we sat round the fire at night, the leader of each group told the story of his march. We had all set out the week before after the fortnight's Bible school, a little uncertain of what was going to happen; now we found what everyone finds, who sets out in the name of his Lord. He lifted us up, and we rejoiced, because our names were written in Heaven.

One after another the stories were told; James led off, "We found the word of God strong in our mouths, and when we preached at night, it slept in the ears of the people, so that they came back in the morning to give themselves up. We came like the Arabs long ago, taking many prisoners, but we bound them with the yoke of Jesus and we left them to do His service in their own homes."

Ngwewa, from the South, was so excited he had to stand up and enact the story before our eyes. He told us how many had turned their backs on the City of Destruction, and borne bravely the mockery of their neighbours. "Perhaps most," he said, "still carry the burden of their sin, but we have pointed out the light that shines above the wicket gate. Their feet are in The Way."

Jonah, from the West, had met with indifference and apathy, but in thirteen villages, the Word had been faithfully declared. Though they had wiped the dust off their feet against some people, yet they knew that the Kingdom of God had come nigh unto them. Our morale was high as we gathered the next morning for the prayer meeting. All night there had been drumming and dancing at the village beer-drink, but when their bawdy songs disturbed our prayers, we burst out singing and our hymns prevailed. The preaching that Sunday bit deep. It was a call for decision. In the name of Christ, James made the demand, "Today you choose. Either you join the army of Christ, which means baptism unto the remission of sins and membership in the church, or you fight against us, using every device that Satan puts into your hands: drunkenness, ignorance, sloth and filth." That day we called the people to remember that sixty years ago their grandfathers had taken up their spears to defend their homes and their cattle against Lewanika and his Barotse hordes. Today they heard again the call to arms, "Put on the whole armour of God and stand!"

Then for eleven months until August comes again, we must carry on the unspectacular work of establishing the churches in the faith. The people must be instructed in the catechism, they must be taught to sing and read with understanding, the Word of God. As fishers of men we not only cast the dragnet into the sea, but when it is drawn up on the shore, we are God's agents in the sorting of the fish. The circuit evangelist can never rest; in all weathers he is out on his bicycle, visiting the churches in the villages. There are books to be distributed to those who can read, and the illiterate must be encouraged to learn. Not every village can be visited every week, so a letter has to be prepared, duplicated, and sent out to the village leaders to give them guidance and encouragement. The quarterly class money must be collected and the class tickets[3] written out.

---

3 Class tickets were given out quarterly by the minister to those who had attended the class meetings. They were paid for; this was one way of collecting money for the church.

When the pioneer missionaries came out, they found that before they could even begin to plough they had to clear the bush. Even when the land is under cultivation, it has to be ploughed and cross-ploughed to keep it in good heart. Even when the seeds are planted, they have to be watered. Our need here is still for ploughmen, but the land is rich and the harvest will be plenteous.

Preaching at Mono village

James Mulala as Superintendent

"On the whole we had a good Synod. We made one very important step forward and appointed our first African Superintendent Minister. I am to be the second man in the Keembe circuit and James Mulala is to be the Superintendent. It is going to mean quite a lot of patience, but I don't see why the European missionaries should have the privilege of making all the mistakes." *January 1951*

Prayers for Enoch's orphans

"When I was teaching at the Kafue Training Institute in 1944, one of our teachers named Enoch died suddenly. According to African custom his relatives came from his village and took his three children away from his wife Annie, leaving her a sadly grieving mother. However hard we pleaded with them, they continued to refuse to return the children. Then quite unexpectedly the elder brother came to see me with a strange request: "We in our village want to send the eldest girl to the Girls' School at Chipembi." We have now found the fees and she has started there. We must continue to pray for the other two children.

"One thing that I am quite sure about, is that by writing these letters to you I have been made to trust less in the appearance of what we so glibly call success and failure, and learnt to rely more on the secret forces of the Spirit that are silently at work within the church. All our class meetings now end up as prayer meetings, and we are learning that to intercede for others is the most significant part of our fellowship." *Prayer Letter 2: September 1950*

The challenge of disciplining the faithful

"Looking back over the months since I last wrote, our life at Nambala seems like a journey across a dry plain. The days that stand out in our memory are the ones when we reached a water-hole and found rest and refreshment, but if I write of these, it does not mean there have not been long, thirsty treks between. More than once I seem to have drained the last drop from my little water bottle, but miraculously there is always a little drop more; perhaps it is your prayer that makes it so.

"Now the Evil One, as though to prove that He has not been entirely vanquished, has struck again. At the Leaders' Meeting in June, there were six names before us for discipline; men and women in whom the flesh had overcome the Spirit. Whenever we missionaries get together the conversation inevitably comes round to this, our most pressing problem—the failure of our African Christians to maintain the high standard of morality that we demand. Again and again we ask ourselves whether we are not expecting too much of a people so newly won from heathenism. Is there not perhaps some intermediate stage through which they can go? But in the end we have to come back to the truth that "God is faithful who will not suffer you to be tempted beyond what you are able; but will, with the temptation, also make the way of escape that you may be able to endure it." The magnitude of the temptation that besets the path of the African Christian challenges us to give them a faith equal to their need. When they fail it is a measure of our own failure in love and prayer for them.

". . . Miss Huntley, the principal of Chipembi Girls' School, has been visiting us this month and as I talked with her I realised that this problem is particularly acute at Chipembi. In African life every girl is expected to marry very soon after the age of puberty. The prospect of marriage fills a girl's whole horizon from a very early age. The educational standard we now expect, demands that a girl puts out of her mind all thought of marriage till she is trained. It is this tension between what the school demands in term time, and what African custom expects in the holidays, that underlies the struggle for women's education in Chipembi. It is here that your prayers for the girls and young teachers can make its most telling impact. This is the kind of prayer that we ask the girls to make: "Oh Lord, so fill my vision with Thy Glory that I become blind to all things else. Let there be no spilling of my cup until Thou has filled it full." *Prayer Letter 4: July 1951*

I keep going with a seemingly impossible task

"This morning I was out choosing the camp site for the Ministerial Retreat, which is to be held here in June, when we missionaries and the African ministers will bend our minds to the question "What is Evangelism?" because at this point in the Mission to Africa we need, above all else, Guidance in our thinking about the fundamentals of our evangelistic task.

"When I look at it, the harvest seems a very meagre one. A handful of stalwart Christians who have kept the faith, a string of schools that serve perhaps 25% of the children in the area, a Mission Station, a hymn book and the New Testament in the vernacular; but I look in vain for the Church—an indigenous church that has discovered at its own risk and responsibility what it really means to be the Church—a community in subjection to Christ and His Spirit, called to fulfil His ministry in the world by its confession of faith, its special quality of life and witness . . . It is trite to say that we need the Holy Spirit to visit us, and yet I ask you to pray for that.

". . . I have been perplexed almost to despair about the work during these past weeks. Is it just because the soil is arid that we reap such a poor crop, or is our method of cultivation wrong? Each day my faith grew smaller against the seeming impossibility of the task; then, early one morning when the house was asleep, I lit my lamp and opened my Bible to read the story of Abraham's faith. There on the page were words I had underlined in my college days: "is there anything too hard for the Lord?" So I have gone on teaching Willie's wife to read, even though it seems impossible that she will ever get beyond page one of the primer; the farm will yet be made to pay, even though Cephas has broken the tractor plough and an ox has died, and the church members who are brewing *intongo* in the villages will repent of it." *Prayer Letter 6: May 1952*

Africans to take on more responsibility

"Never have we had a synod with so many big problems to face, one of them being the serious situation that has arisen in the Rural Circuits. We have four rural stations and only two senior men able to take them on. There are new men coming out but they have not yet got the language or sufficient experience. There was a strong move to put me at Masuku where a situation has arisen in the Zambezi valley which calls for some very drastic measures. For over a week we have been producing draft after

Early days in Nambala: Audrey (in hat) with the Sisterhood, the local Methodist women's fellowship.

draft of stations and I was alternately at Nambala and Masuku. At the moment I feel like a deflated football, but the final decision is that I continue at Nambala for another year to crystallise my plans for that Circuit. Next year I may go to Masuku; I should love to tackle the work in the Zambezi valley—it is the most thrilling job on our field." *January 1953*

Visiting the village schools

"I have just got back from a week's tour round the villages on my bicycle. The purpose of my tour was to visit the village schools and inspect their work. It was very depressing to find how little progress the children make, and how unwillingly they come to school. Everything really depends on the character of the teacher, especially on his conscientiousness. How few men of strong character there seem to be. Unless a man has got lots of guts, even with ten years' training in a Christian school, he soon slips back into the happy-go-lucky life of the villages. Then of course the school just peters out." *April 1953*

Pulled in two directions

"I was at Mpili last week to see about the building of the new Girls' School there, and I found that Mr Mulala had called in some of his people for two days of prayer and preparation before they set out on a preaching campaign through the villages. I longed to go with them, but I had to spend the day arguing about the wages to be paid the builders, and wondering how to cut the cost of making bricks with a labour force which recorded a steady daily absentee rate of 60%. I have asked you before to pray for laymen to come out and help us here, and these past months I have never felt the need more urgent. In this land, where the old African society has disintegrated and where the re-building has to start below the old foundations, our Mission must be there working alongside Government and all other agencies in the tremendous task of reconstruction . . . The trouble is that our witness is greatly weakened by the fact that the minister is constantly being deflected from the task to which he is peculiarly called, so that he can sustain the fight in some other sector where a skilled artisan or educationist should be leading the troops.

"I think I speak for many of my colleagues when I say that this is the tension more than any other that wears us down. If I go to the Sala to preach I know that the bricks are being badly made at Mpili, and that the cost is going to soar above the estimate; if I am at Mpili sitting by the kiln, an evangelist is falling into temptation in the Sala because he has not got the sustaining fellowship of his minister. The tragedy is that while we Europeans are trying to do the double work of the ministry and the laity we are setting a wrong example, both to the African ministers and the African laity. I have come to see that it is as necessary to give time and thought to the training of Circuit stewards and Society stewards as it is to train the ordained ministry . . . The need is still urgent for dedicated laymen." *Prayer Letter 9: July 1953*

The way ahead

"Last week I went to Lusaka for a district committee and got the chance for a long talk with Mr. Beetham, the Mission House Africa Secretary. I think he would like to see us getting on more quickly with the handing over of responsibility to the African ministers. I only hope he will not mince matters when he writes his report. It gives me hope when I think we have got a man like that at Mission Headquarters. He is making all new missionaries do a course at the School of Oriental and African Studies before sailing, and insists that the probationers Boyer and Jenkin must be free from responsibility for the first eighteen months to get on with the language." *October 1953*

"We are all safely home again from Synod, and Boyer is with us for a few days more until he goes out to Mpili for six months to work under James Mulala. It has been a very controversial synod and I have found myself as the self-appointed leader of the opposition. It is not a role I enjoy, because it so often happens that when you attack a principle, you seem to be attacking the men who support it. Often I was quite alone in the stand I made, and my only comfort was that I believed if Beetham had been there he would have supported me. I stopped short of a real showdown, but I have shown my colours and I am afraid that next time the real clash will come." *January 1954*

A final tour of the villages

"I am just back from a week's visit to the Keembe schools. September is my favourite month in the bush for it is our 'springtime'. In the Mutundo tree country the new leaves on the trees are crimson and pale green, and with the evening sunlight shining through them they make the usually monotonous forest land as beautiful as any English beech wood.

"As well as inspecting the schools I had to tour the surrounding villages to try and get the children back to school. I found that a number of girls aged between twelve and fourteen had married during the school holidays, and of course there was the usual exodus of boys from the villages to the towns. In these schools the attendance is about 50% of the roll, and the roll 50% of what it ought to be. The people are a long way yet from having a hunger for education. However I have been lucky to get hold of an African contractor to finish the building of the girls' school at Mpili. He is from Nyasaland; how I wish I had found him three years ago.

"The educational work is now so interesting and absorbing I find it hard to turn my mind to anything else, except the thought of furlough which is my constant preoccupation in my leisure moments." *October 1954*

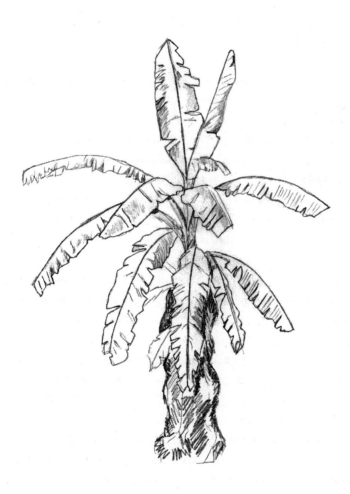

Nambala: Preaching Farmers

ON THE MISSION STATION we have a dispensary and we give treatment to all who come. Those whom we are unable to treat, and who will dare to go to town on the mail lorry, can be sent to the Lusaka hospital, a hundred and thirty miles away. There is a constant stream of people with coughs, colds, cuts and bruises. Occasionally a man with snakebite will be sent to hospital for an injection of the special serum. Battered heads, spear wounds and even gunshot wounds are not uncommon, especially in the last months of the dry season after the harvest, a time when in some villages the beer drinking is continuous . . . We are always thankful that we have the means to alleviate much pain; sometimes we have been able to save life, but we know all too well that it is rescue work. The root of sickness and disease among the people lies in the conditions under which they live, their ignorance of the simplest rules of hygiene, the poverty of their diet and the immoral customs which they practise.

In order to meet these basic needs, and to provide a type of training that would prepare men and women to lead their people on to a higher standard of living, we started what we call a Village Craft School. We set out our aims as follows:-

1. To encourage the youth of the District to get established on the land, or in some other worthwhile rural occupation, and take a responsible part in the welfare and development of the community to which they belong.

2. To provide training in sound rural practices for selected families, who can then return to their communities to serve as basic family units for important projects to be started in their areas.

With the financial backing of the Commissioner of Native Development and with the help of the District Commissioner and the Chiefs, we started with twenty young men, most of whom have passed Standard IV (six years of education) some time during the last five years, but had never found a permanent occupation. They were a very mixed lot. The older men brought with them their wives and families. We built a village of thatched houses for them to live in on the mission station, and they have entered into their new life with some enthusiasm. They have two hours a day in the classroom learning simple English, account keeping, civics, building theory and singing.

They are divided into three groups and each takes its turn at building, carpentry and gardening. Each group in turn built a house using local materials: the kind of house a man could build for himself in his village. In the carpenter's shop each man makes a door for his own house and shutters for the windows from locally sawn timber. As timber has been available they have made beds, tables and chairs. Irrigating a small garden with a hand-pump from a shallow well, they have grown a good deal of their own food in the way of vegetables, and in a demonstration plot they will plant a rotation of beans, potatoes, groundnuts and maize.

The women will run their own homes, which are inspected each week, and attend some lectures in hygiene, baby care and cooking. They spend most afternoons learning to sew and make their own school uniform. Those who are illiterate are given opportunities to learn to read and write. The experiment is still in its early stages and we have yet to see how these young men and women will fare when they return to their villages. We believe it is an experiment worth making and although at present on only a very small scale, under a qualified layman it could develop a far-reaching influence on the life of the rural community. [1]

My vision begins to be a reality

"At the moment we are on the crest of a wave, and busier than we have ever been. It has been my dream that our mission station should be the centre of the religious and cultural life of our area. This morning I felt it was beginning to be so. On the football pitch there were 60 village chil-

1 *The Widening Way,* p. 26-7

dren doing their P.T. before going into school; six apprentices were working on our new building, six were making doors in the carpenter's shop and six were irrigating in the vegetable garden. People were coming along the roads for treatment at the dispensary and in the church I had 20 villagers for Bible study. Half of these were the new converts from our campaign—they have come in for three days to learn the tunes of the hymns in our new village hymn book. Our Senior Evangelist, James Ngwewa, who wrote the hymns, is here to teach them. It is funny to think how much the child is the father of the man. The things I am doing now, P.T., gardening, carpentry and preaching, I was doing at Earnseat." *September 1948*

Audrey's medical work

"Audrey has had to deal with four medical emergencies this week—a broken leg, a broken arm, an abdominal problem and a woman brought in after four days in labour with twins. Sadly the first two cases died; however the District Commissioner offered us his vanette and his driver so the mother and the broken arm case were rushed into Lusaka. I am having a battle with the Provincial Medical Officer about funds for the dispensary. At present the Government gives us £100 and our Society puts in £200 —the figures ought to be reversed. I am also having a running fight with the District Commissioner about funds for our Rural Training course. Sometimes I wish I could cut adrift entirely from government financial aid and be independent." *February 1949*

An ox with an Irish name

"I had a letter to say that Drumshambo had sent £5 for work at Nambala. I have to write and thank them for the gift and specify the use to which I will put it. I am going to buy an ox for our plough team and call it Drumshambo; it will give me great delight to hear the herd boy shouting 'Yo, Drumshambo—kwela! kwela!' when he is out ploughing on the lands." *August 1950*

Time Kabumbwe, our home-grown vegetable gardener

"We are going all out for agriculture this year. We had the Deputy Director of Agriculture here this week and we are getting his department's help in laying out here a model peasant's holding. We may even be able to borrow a Ferguson to help with the ploughing. If only we can make the land pay, one day my dream of a Ferguson of my own may come true. The

school irrigated garden is beginning to look green and I am very pleased because one of the first boys who came here for training, and whom we regarded as the school dunce, has now become our garden instructor. I go down in the morning and find him lovingly pinching out the laterals on the tomato plants or looking worried because the spinach seedlings are damping off. I long to get the boys to love the soil—most of them think of nothing but a good job on the mines. Time Kabumbwe (that is his name) takes great pride in knowing the names of his vegetables and insists that his boys shall learn them too. One of the boys this year is deaf and sometimes I hear Time's voice floating up from the garden as he yells into Tembo's straining ear: 'Shorthorn carrot, Drumhead cabbage, Canadian Wonder beans!'" *1st September 1950*

The mathematics of subsistence

"To a people who practise only subsistence agriculture, one of our great battles is to get them to understand that they can make a living out of the land. One day a week I do some arithmetic with the boys, which goes something like this: 'This morning I have 5 potatoes – 1lb which cost me 4d at the Indian store – we plant them – the rain comes and we dig them

– now we have 50 potatoes, which we sell to the District Commissioner at 4d per lb,' and the boys' eyes grow round with wonder when they see the profits to be made." *September 1950*

An African 'green house'

"It is Time Kabumbwe who saves me from despair. (I baptised him Saul last year but I can never to remember to give him his proper name). I lent him a book called 'How to grow better vegetables' and yesterday I asked him how he was getting on with it. He said it made him ashamed (a) because our garden beds were not laid out as the diagram in the book, and (b) because we had no greenhouse to keep the tools in; then he took me to see the 'green house' he and his boys were building out of poles and grass." *September 1950*

A tractor to beat the tsetse fly

"It is very good of Mrs Barnes to want to send something for the 'farm'. Both our pigs died the other day: tsetse fly, so our prospects of getting cattle are not very hopeful. I think I am going quietly to start my own private tractor fund—it is quite against the rules, but I shall have to make the exception which will prove the rule." *November 1950*

A day of disasters

"I am late again with my letter and in no mood to be writing home to you. This has been one of those days when all the heavens seemed to be falling. We got back late last night after our two weeks in Broken Hill. Most of the baby chicks have been allowed to die, only a few of the cattle have arrived and the vet has not brought out the Antrycide injections, one of the young teachers is going to marry Agnes our treasured nurse girl—in short, if I could find a hole in the ground I would crawl into it. I must close now as I have to leave at 4.30 am tomorrow for another two days in the bush—I am leaving a two weeks' accumulation of mail on my desk to answer itself." *August 1951*

A plan for Preaching Farmers

"Some of you may remember how, when I was on deputation, I told you about our evangelistic campaigns and Bible Schools in Nambala. We have not been able to hold the ground we won. I have come to realise more than ever that the stability of the churches in the villages depends far more on the quality of life and depth of faith of local Christian leaders than on any other factor.

"The annual Bible School, which lasts for three weeks, is miserably inadequate to meet their needs. I realise now that it is necessary to get the leaders to live with us in community here, and experience for themselves the meaning of Christian fellowship. Since I returned from furlough we have been making plans to this end and on 1st September this year we start the experiment which I have dreamed about for so long.

"The course of training for leaders will work in with the Rural Train-ing Course (Village Craft School), which I started here three years ago. Let me briefly outline the scheme so that you can support it from the start with your prayers.

"The course of training that we have planned aims to do two things:

1. To enable men to earn an honest living on their farm in their villages. Normally the villager has to spend months away from home working on the mines or in the towns. It has frequently hap-pened that a Christian community has flickered and died because its leader has gone away to earn money for his tax and his wife's clothes.

2. To train leaders to know their Bibles and, above all, to let them experience the joy of living in a community where Christ is Lord. Ten picked men, some of whom were won on the first evangelis-tic campaign, will be coming with their wives to take their place alongside the twenty young men who are here to learn carpentry, building and farming.

"At Nambala we have the land—acres of virgin soil in the fertile Chibila valley. From Colonial Development funds we have obtained grants for bush clearing, tools and salaries for African staff. Through the generosity of Mr Lewis, who has backed my schemes ever since his son and I made a garden from a wilderness when we were boys at school, I have been able to purchase a little walking tractor which will enable the men in training to grow their own food and earn enough, we hope, to buy dresses for their wives.

"There is no villager who cannot earn a good living from the land, once he has the know-how. We are particularly eager to help those who live, as we do, in the tsetse fly belt where, up to the present, all cultivation has had to be done by hand hoe. We are therefore going to conduct three experiments simultaneously: one with the small cooperatively-owned tractor, another with donkeys that are said to be resistant to tsetse fly, and the third with cattle injected with a new drug, Antrycide, which it has been claimed gives immunity to cattle for six months."

The Poultry Club

"We have already begun to experiment with improved poultry-keeping, in the hope that we can train the women in the villages to earn their pin money. At present if they want any money of their own, they brew beer from the kaffir corn which they can sell at a good profit in a ready market. Christian women are debarred from this, and we must give them an alternative method of earning money.

"We are crossing black Australorp and Rhode Island Red cocks with native hens, as black chickens are not easily seen by hawks or eagles. I got the most beautiful Australorp cock from the veterinary department with which to start the poultry improvement scheme. Previously I had inserted an advert in the Lusaka press under the heading '*WANTED: Rhode Island Red cockerels*'. The idiots put it in under '*FOR SALE*', and I was getting orders for dozens of cockerels that didn't exist even in my own imagination. Already the first generation is scampering about my back yard, to the endless delight of my two small daughters.

"Compost from veldt grasses and poultry manure is an integral part of our plan for improved farming. I wish you gardeners could see me taking the temperature of my own little compost heap on a Saturday afternoon. I sometimes wonder whether a Methodist Preacher who, to use John Wesley's dictum, 'has nothing to do but save souls', should be taking such a delight in his chickens and compost heap. Today I was comforted by the daily reading from William Temple, "Our capacity to raise society depends on our being veritable members of it, working for the highest things that we can work for in it, but not cutting ourselves off from it, nor standing aside and giving good advice from the touch-line." *Prayer Letter 4: July 1951*

The first days for the Preaching Farmers

"We made all preparations for the opening of the 'Preaching Farmers' course on 1st September. Everyone was told to be in by sundown on that day, but when I went round the houses in the evening only six men had arrived. Fortunately, by now being familiar with the African concept of time, which is that one day is as good as the next, I was not unduly concerned, though it did look as if most of those who had promised to come had suddenly got cold feet. However a week later there were thirty-five men on parade in the morning; when or how they came I do not know, as it was enough for me that they were there.

"So work began. The first three hours of the day we worked together on the land, cutting out roots and stumps ready for the tractor and oxen to come in with the ploughs. I knew that I could not teach the dignity of labour from the pulpit and that I had to take my own shirt off for that particular lesson. We tried to put the oxen, which we had bought at Chitanda 100 miles away, into the plough, but the villagers of that place must have sold us all the beasts that had been too bad-tempered for them to train. Once we nearly killed the whole herd by giving an overdose of Antrycide. Drumshambo, an ox given to us by the people of that town, behaved as Irish as its name. Another called Lion Spoor caused the herd to stampede, and went off to roam in an area thick with tsetse fly. It was a week before we captured him again. The Africans have given him another name which, when interpreted, means 'Little Demon'."

The walking tractor arrives

"Then the rains came and the little tractor arrived. It is a beautiful machine, and it seemed cruel to put it into the hands of men raw from the bush who had never handled anything mechanical before, but it had to be done. Charles Boyer, my new colleague, and I first learned to use it and then we set out to train others. It was a living parable of all missionary work. You set a fine straight line down the centre of the field, then stand aside to watch an African turn it into snaking curves, then instead of rushing out to snatch the plough from his hand you remind yourself that he will never learn unless you trust him on his own to make his own mistakes. We have found that the tractor, which was designed for market gardeners at home, is too light for ploughing up the virgin bush, but in spite of the difficulties there are now thirty acres of maize springing up, and that means food for a year for the men who come here for training."
Prayer Letter 5: January 1952

The wealth of Africa lies in the soil

"Somehow we have to teach these men that their wealth lies in their own soil, and that the streets of the towns are not paved with gold. By the labour of their hands they can save themselves from the grinding poverty that degrades them, and from the economic servitude to the white population. Only a few yet realise how urgent it is for the people to rise up out of their lethargy and ignorance and make use of the land that is theirs. Unless they do begin to use it, they will lose it. There are land-hungry whites pouring into the country from the south who already cast covetous eyes on these fertile plains. There are many Europeans who believe that the land can only be developed by large-scale mechanical farming. From the point of view of economics and maximum food production they are probably right, but that is not what I came to Africa to do. I came here to help the peasants of the Mumbwa District to plough and plant their own land, not become slave labourers on European farms.

"This is the point where your prayers for us have most value. I can hardly ask you to pray for Drumshambo the Little Demon, nor for the tractor nor the crops, but I do covet the power of your prayer for the peasants who have come here for training.

"Now let me tell you about of some of the men who have come in from the villages to take the Preaching Farmers course.

Zachao Mukalo, the hunter

"We went to Zachao's village in 1947 with a band of preachers on our first evangelistic campaign. I had a magic lantern with me and I showed a coloured film strip of the life of St Paul. During the service a man called

Bernard came out of the darkness into the firelight and knelt to confess his sins. Later he found his brother Zachao and brought him into the church. Zachao was a hunter. He used to go out after bush pig and buck with his old muzzle loader. I met him one day on one of the bush paths and expressed my surprise that he had no gun with him. He laughed and said, 'I have replaced my gun with my New Testament. I am going to preach in Suzu's village where I have a class of eight members meeting there.' Zachao was baptised last year and now, after his work on the farm in the morning, he sits for two hours in the classroom learning to understand the Bible.

Howard Milupi, the blind man

"Howard is a young man who five years ago went blind. In the misery of the first months of his blindness, he quarrelled with his brother and stabbed him in the darkness with a penknife. I was called in by the father to settle the case. Howard has travelled a long way since then, and last year I baptised him. He asked to attend the Bible classes. When the others were copying notes from the blackboard, I sat with him and taught him the scripture references orally. I soon found that he had a retentive memory, and before long he was taking services in the villages and reading a lesson from memory.

"Then the chance came to send him to a school for the blind at Magwero 400 miles away in the Eastern Province where he learned Braille. He had set his heart on becoming an evangelist. At first we prayed that he would receive his sight, but now we are praying that his vision may be enlarged, for it seems God may use him even more mightily as a blind preacher than as one who has eyes to see. In the cold nights of winter, when the villagers huddle round their little fires in the darkness, his nimble fingers slide along the pages of his Braille Bible as Howard reads to them the Word of God." *Prayer Letter 5: January 1952*

News of Willie Mpatiwa, our carpenter

"Willie is going through a particularly difficult time at present. If I tell you about him it will give you some understanding of what our young Christians are up against when they marry according to native custom. Your prayers for the building up of Christian homes in Africa will have point and significance as you pray for him. Four years ago he decided that the time had come for him to get married, so he went to his people and asked them to find a wife. A girl was found and the first instalment of the *lobola* (dowry) was paid with the understanding that if the marriage proved successful the final payment would be made in due course. This custom of trial marriage means that the woman suffers from a terrible sense of insecurity during the early days of her marriage, knowing that the man may cast her off at the slightest provocation.

"Insecurity leads to jealousies. It means that the husband starts out in marriage with the idea that his wife is there to pleasure him and that if she does not do so he will send her home and find another. Willie's wife is illiterate and when she sees her husband writing letters she is jealous lest he be writing to find another woman to take her place. Last week they had a quarrel and fought it out, literally tooth and nail. If Willie was not a Christian that would certainly be the end of the marriage, but we have talked it out and there is a chance that the broken pieces may be gathered together and a new beginning made. That is what we are praying for." *Prayer Letter 5: January 1952*

Demas and Zimilie as pioneers

"I have news for you of Demas and Zimilie. For a long time as a member of the Area Development team I have been urging the Government to start a peasant farming scheme to settle people on the land. News came through not long ago from the Provincial Commissioner that a thousand pounds had been granted to lay out an experimental peasant farming block; to clear the bush, purchase cattle and implements and settle twenty families on the land and teach them to use sound agricultural practices such as soil conservation and rotation of crops . . .

"Early one morning this week thirty of us set off with our axes from Nambala to walk the three miles up the Chibila valley to the place where the Agricultural Officer is marking out the contours and laying out the farm plots. Demas has chosen his plot and we went out to help him cut the poles for the new house which he will have to build himself. Later on I hope the women of the Sisterhood will go out to cut the grass for the thatch; in Africa grass cutting is women's work. Demas is leaving his salaried employment in the Mission to take up this farming; we hope he is going to lead the way into a new manner of life for his people, and form the nucleus of a Christian church amongst the farmers. Pray for him and Zimilie, that they will have strength for their toil and faith for their pioneer work." *Prayer Letter 6: May 1952*

A farmer's life

"I seem to be living a very secular life these past few weeks. The little tractor has been working full blast to get all the maize shelled, and even though I know nothing about machines, it is more than my African staff know, so I am constantly being called out to put things right when they go wrong. Rodwell Pali is away, so now I have to see to the injections of cattle myself." *June 1953*

The Mumbwa Show

"I have been preparing the exhibit for the Mumbwa show. We want to demonstrate how all our work stems from the Bible. We are putting an open Bible in the centre of our display with tapes running out from key texts to examples of our work. 'Till the garden and keep it' is demonstrated by maize cobs, beans, pawpaws, carrots, groundnuts etcetera, grown at Nambala. 'Work with quietness and earn your own living' goes to a stool made by our carpenters and the brickwork of our builders. A table with a white cloth demonstrates, 'Do this in remembrance of me'. It is the first time we have tried anything of this kind and I only hope it will be understood. At least Jukes Curtis, our charming but canny local trader, gets the point as he calls me 'the missionary with a Bible in one hand and a plough in the other'." *June 1953*

Demas and Zimilie struggle

"The new peasant farming scheme has run into heavy weather; three of the men who started have given up. Their houses have never been finished and remain derelict skeletons of poles and reeds. Demas has battled on and, in spite of a serious veldt fire, he has managed to find enough grass to get the roof thatched and Rodwell Pali went out to help him put the roof on. Zimilie went home to see her mother, a 500 mile journey by road and rail. At Kasempa she fell ill, and the last news we have is that she is in hospital there. We pray for her recovery and speedy return.

Willie Mpatiwa moving on

"Willie's wife has had a second child and I believe that their marriage is going to last. But I am fearful, because this month Willie came to say that he is going to leave Nambala. He has found that the salary he gets here as an Instructor is less than he would get working for a building contractor in one of the towns. Willie is young and ambitious, and the shops are full of things he wants to buy. I shall be sorry to see him go, for I doubt if the Carpenter's shop will ever be as happy as it was under him. He needs your prayers more now than ever before as he leaves the shelter of our little community for the bleak life of the towns." *Prayer Letter 7: September 1952*

A tropical jungle

"I have just arrived home after being away for three weeks for the audit and the Synod. You know what a suburban garden looks like when you return to it after a summer holiday? Well, Nambala after three weeks away is a tropical jungle. The maize is standing in the fields over nine feet tall, while the road over the Chibila embankment is a tunnel through the grass and dangerously slippery. The cattle kraal is a quagmire, and the herd is stricken with foot and mouth disease; fortunately we do not have to slaughter them in this country and I hope they will recover, though it means we are without milk again and no ploughing can be done." *Prayer Letter 10: January 1954*

A fair deal for women?

"I am busy trying to persuade people to switch our Nambala Rural Training Scheme from men to women. I am becoming more feminist than the W.D.[2] African women are not getting a square deal, and I am sure that is why we make so little progress. I want Nambala to become a 'Homecraft Centre' for training village women and girls. Unfortunately I shall not be here to see it through, but I have learnt that you have to talk about a thing for at least three years in this country before you can get anything done." *February 1954*

Our farm finally bears fruit

"I have often told you how I have been battling to persuade our people that their economic salvation lies in their own hands and that God is as much concerned with their sinful neglect of their soil as with their drunkenness and indolence. You remember how we started an experimental farm and how we introduced the first herd of cattle into tsetse fly country? Until a few months ago, although our demonstration farm was doing well, we seemed to be making no impression on the people round about

2 The Women's Division of the UK Methodist Church

who continued in their old ways. Then suddenly the dam wall of their indifference broke, the village people began driving in their cattle from the Kafue flats and three of them bought their own ploughs. A week ago I stood and watched Chief Mono ploughing with his own oxen in his own fields—that for me was something of a miracle.

Farewells to the people of Nambala

"There are now only six weeks before I sail for home. And I am about to say goodbye to Nambala, the people with whom I have worked, the oxen in the kraal, the house we built, and the hill whence cometh my strength. I have asked for your prayers for the work here. We have had our disappointments: Willie went off to the Line;[3] Saul, who showed such promise, has withered in the bud; Demas and Zimilie have broken up their home; but others have come forward to fill the gaps in the ranks. Sam Luwisha has carried on faithfully; Rodwell, whom I doubted would stay the course, has kept faith with us and is doing fine work on the farm. James Cholobesha, who first drifted away to the Line, came back again and is now Sam's assistant in the shop and has been given a note to preach." *Prayer Letter 11: January 1955*

---

3 The Line of Rail. See note on p. 52

Winds of Change 8

The Africans' fears that their land will be stolen

IN OUR RURAL ISOLATION we were unaware of the 'winds of change' which were beginning to sweep across Africa, but I was becoming aware of how deeply resentful the people were of the coming of the white man to take up farms along the Line of Rail.

I had an indication of the depth of their fears when the government's Department of Water Affairs sent a white water engineer to supervise teams of well-diggers in the villages. It was a three-year programme so this man, who had a wife and child, decided to build a small thatched house from sun-dried brick rather than live in a tent. The rumour quickly spread that he was a government spy, who had been sent to find out where there was good land that would be given to white settlers.

As part of a programme of land conservation to prevent soil erosion, the government helped African peasant farmers to construct contour ridges. It started well, but again a rumour began to spread that once the peasants had made the ridges, Boer farmers would move in to take the land. Chief Shakumbila's area south of the Mission was the worst affected, and as I was manager of a primary school near the chief's court and knew him well, I was sent to quash this rumour, along with Unwin Moffat the provincial agricultural officer. A big meeting was called. The Chief sat on his stool in the shade of a giant wild fig tree, with 150 peasant farmers gathered round him seated on the ground. They had come on their bicycles which they parked under the surrounding trees, but not before they had taken care to remove the bicycle pumps from the clips under the cross bars and stuff them down the backs of their shirts with the pump handles protruding at the neck.

Through the official government interpreter, Unwin Moffat explained how important it was to continue making contour ridges, because otherwise all the top soil would be washed away, and it would not be possible to grow any food crops at all. He said that for the good of the people the government had introduced a Native Authority Ordinance, which would force all farmers to make ridges and keep them in good repair. If they refused to do so Chief Shakumbila would impose a heavy fine.

When he had finished his speech Moffat sat down by the side of the Chief. There was silence at first, then the farmers began to mutter amongst themselves and the muttering swelled into an angry chorus of dissent. Then to a man they all stood up, and drawing their cycle pumps from their shirt collars like bayonets from their scabbards, they waved them in the air shouting *"Twakaka, twakaka.* We refuse, we refuse." They gathered up their cycles from under the trees and rode away, leaving the Chief, Unwin Moffat and me to reflect on the Sala's defiant audacity and the government's total impotence in the face of it.

"There must be political trouble-makers abroad," said the District Commissioner when we returned to the Boma.

A district development plan

"On Wednesday we had a big meeting to prepare the first coherent Development Plan for the District. The Provincial Commissioner and Commissioner for Native Development were present as well as technical staff. The main idea is to move the population out of the tsetse infected areas and settle each family on a forty-acre farm. The first pilot scheme of twenty men is to start this year at a place only four miles from here. I'm hoping to get some of our Nambala men to start the thing going. For once the mission has been one step ahead of Government. My part in the scheme is to act as a buffer between the Provincial Administration and the people who are terribly suspicious of anything new. For years the Government has forced the people to pay taxes, now when they come offering gifts of land and cattle to help the people, of course they are suspicious. It sounds so sensible to us Europeans, but to uproot a man from his ancestral lands is a hard thing. First comes the Game and Tsetse Department with their gangs to clear the bush and fight back the fly on the fringes, then the Medical Department to screen all the people who move from sleeping sickness areas. The Water Development Department come in to make new wells and dams and weirs; the Agricultural Department to put in contour ridges and mark out the farm plots, the Vets to inject the cattle and the District Commissioner to co-ordinate the whole thing. The missionary knows that unless the people can get a new vision of community life, the whole thing will be a failure. It is a great help to me that Chief Mono, in whose area the scheme starts, is a personal friend of mine. Already we have spent many hours talking the thing out; we know you can't explain things to illiterate people by broadsheets and pamphlets. What matters is patient negotiation." *February 1952*

The poisoned sugar rumour

"The African National Congress (ANC) has been active in our area. I felt it necessary to warn our teachers that if they join this party they should do so with their eyes open, whereupon I received a letter from the local organizing secretary of ANC which was quite an eye-opener. The ANC has led the fight against Federation, but unfortunately they do not stop there. They have spread the poisoned sugar story, that anyone eating sugar produced by Europeans will become sterile. I personally hope that the Federation plan will go through, as I think all this talk about African opposition to it is a lot of nonsense. If it does go through I think we're in for some trouble. I very much doubt if it will be BIG trouble because I don't think the Africans here have sufficient guts to put up a fight, but funny things happen when hot-headed Nationalists get talking in the villages. I speak about these things to our local Chief Mono and his reply is: "I am not stopping eating sugar because I don't want any more children anyway." *March 1953*

Federation and the Northern Rhodesian villager

I wrote an article in early 1953 for *Young Britain*[1].

Last Sunday I cycled out seventeen miles into the bush from my station, to take my preaching appointment. After the service was over I sat with the village schoolteacher on the veranda of his house. We chewed sugar cane and talked. With him was the foreman of a labour gang which was clearing land for a new seed farm, an Agricultural Assistant and a few

---

1 *Young Britain* was a monthly four-page youth supplement, incorporated into the *Methodist Recorder*. Reproduced by permission.

villagers. They told me they had stopped buying sugar from the stores, because they had heard a rumour that all sugar sold after 1 February, that is after the Federation talks in London, would be poisoned by the Europeans. It was a secret and mysterious poison that did not kill the individual, but would ultimately exterminate the African race by preventing women from bearing children. I had heard some time before that this rumour was being spread by some clever person who wanted to destroy race relations, and who knew all too well how to play on the fears and superstitions of the Africans, but I was taken aback by the readiness with which my friends implicitly believed this fantastic story. Three of them at least were what we might call 'educated Africans'. I heard the next day that all the boys in a big Government boarding school had stopped taking sugar on their porridge for the same reason. This incident gives some indication of the suspicion there is in the minds of Africans towards the Europeans in this country.

Last year the Governor issued a statement on 'partnership' and it was sent round to the native authorities for discussion. I spoke to one of the Chiefs afterwards and asked him what he thought of the new policy as I myself was impressed. His reply was interesting. "It is only a new word for an old thing," he said. "I wonder why the Governor asked us to talk about friendship between black and white as a new thing, for it is an old thing which is now passing away. We know that the Government is doing many good things for us—schools and wells and hospitals, but the men who do these things for us are not our friends in the same way as they used to be. I remember the time when the District Commissioner went through all my villages on foot. We had time to get news of his coming, he talked to us in our own language, and there was one who even wrote a book about our customs. But today they never stay long in one place, they never have time to learn the language, and they always have much work in the Boma offices. And you missionaries if you are not careful will be the same. We liked you better before you had your cars."

I did my best to explain that times were changing, that the days of the ox-wagon were no more, and we are forced to move with the times, whether we like it or not. But I do not think he was listening. As for his people, personal relationships mattered more than economic progress. And so it is that when we come to talk about Federation with the people, they cannot discuss the proposals on their merits, but say quite simply, "We don't want Federation because we don't trust you white people who want to bring it about."

Whether Federation comes or not, this deep distrust of the European by the African will remain, unless we who believe in partnership dispel it. The situation in Northern Rhodesia could be revolutionised if a hundred young men and women would give up their security and their 'prospects' and set sail for central Africa, believing in partnership because they believe in Christ. Why don't you come, you who are teachers and farmers, and carpenters, doctors and nurses, junior clerks and architects? As well as ordinary missionaries we need a dedicated band of 'tent makers' who will come out here in secular employment, to work alongside the Africans and demonstrate in daily life what partnership really means.

The missionary as bible grease

One afternoon Audrey and I were having tea in the shade of the big fig-tree in our front garden. Sunday afternoon is a time when our privacy is respected and no-one comes knocking on our doors. If there is a real emergency, whoever comes will walk down the garden path through the archway and the grapefruit trees to the house.

Suddenly a man appeared from the forest on our southern border. He was dressed in an old khaki shirt and shorts to match. He gave no greeting. He just walked up to me and handed me a pencilled note written on a page torn from an exercise book.

"Dear *Muluti*. You are a missionary put here by the Government to apply Bible Grease but I want to tell you that the time is coming when you and all White people in our country will be chased away." There was no signature.

He turned away and went back through the trees of the forest from whence he came, leaving me to ponder on the phrase 'Bible grease'. Then the penny dropped. The word for grease in Ci-Ila is *mafuta*. It is the word used by farmers for the grease that they smear on the shoulders of the oxen when they yoke them to the plough. I said to myself, "So that is what he means: the Government is using us missionaries to smear grease on the shoulders of the Africans, believing that the Bible will keep them soft, making them accept the heavy yoke of colonial rule."

The next day I went to the Mumbwa Show. The Colonial Governor came out from Lusaka to show the flag. All the chiefs and their councillors gathered to welcome the Governor. They were an unimpressive group of men dressed up in ill-fitting secondhand lounge suits, wearing a variety of hats from bowlers to feather-bedecked trilbies. The only exception was Chief Chibuluma who wore his traditional leopard skins. The governor in his gleaming white uniform with gold braided epaulettes and plumed helmet was an imposing figure. He was accompanied by the silver band of the Northern Rhodesia Police, and when they struck up the strains of "God Save The Queen" the District Commissioner and I stood shoulder to shoulder with him on the show ground dais.

After the opening ceremony I wandered off to mingle with the crowds, and behind one of the hastily-erected stalls I was accosted once again by the man who had called me a Bible greaser. This time he delivered, not a letter, but a small brown paper parcel, which felt almost like a bag of coins, but was too light to be money. I tore it open and saw the glitter of about a hundred gilded tokens which I recognised as the little medals, which I as Manager of Schools had issued for distribution to all children in our mission schools to commemorate the coronation of Queen Elizabeth II. How the children were supposed to pin them on if they wore no shirts, I do not know.

Then the man spoke to me and said, "We are telling you to take back these medals to your Queen in England and tell her that we do not recognise her as our ruler. Mr. Harry Nkumbula, the National President of the African National Congress of Northern Rhodesia, is the true leader of this country."

Then he disappeared into the crowd, and I was left holding the medals in my hand and wondering what I should do. One of the Governor's staff then came to tell me that it was my turn to meet this august gentleman for an informal chat about the work of the Methodist Mission in the District. I told the Governor about the return of the medals; after all, he was the Queen's representative and would know what should be done about such a horrendous insult.

But he seemed to laugh it off. "Don't worry, young man," he said, "I've heard that there are one or two of these chaps around who are beginning to get a bit too big for their boots. You don't need to concern yourself;

I can assure you we have the situation totally under control. I'll ask the District Commissioner to get his messengers to find out who this chap is and we'll make arrangements to have him followed. We'll soon put a stop to all this nonsense."

Many years later I was to learn that my mysterious visitor was Edward Liso Mungoni, who became one of Zambia's most highly respected politicians and a member of the Anglican Church.

The Federation issue polarizes black and white

"I hesitate to say anything about the political scene, for it is all so confused, yet you must have all been reading about Mr. Attlee's visit in the English press, and will realize that Federation is being taken very seriously by the British Parliament. The President and the Secretary of the African Congress, which is leading the fight against Federation, are both products of our Methodist schools, and before they became politicians were Mission teachers. Whether Federation will be to the ultimate advantage of the African is a subject of divided opinion, although personally I think it will be. But the real issue is whether it will be forced through by the British Government in the face of African opposition, and whether this opposition to it is real or merely manufactured by a few politically-minded Africans.

"Whether justified or not, there is a deep distrust amongst Africans of any proposal made by Europeans for their benefit. To think of the dispute in terms of either 'Downtrodden Natives protest against domination by White settlers' or 'Gallant white Pioneers defend Democracy against Black demagogues' is of course a dangerous oversimplification. One thing is certain, and that is that moderate European opinion is being alienated by the unreasonable attitude of the African leaders, who prefer to shout defiance rather than discuss this problem. Our Chairman, the Rev. E. G. Nightingale, who represents African interests in the Legislative Council, with Mr. John Moffat, the great grandson of Robert Moffat, need your constant prayer as they try to bring Christian principles to bear on decisions that will have far reaching consequences for the future. For good or ill Black and White have got to work out their salvation together in this land. The future belongs to neither race alone, but to a partnership."
Prayer letter 7: September 1952

African opposition to Federation

"I see such a lot of nonsense written about the African opposition to Federation. Even the Christian Council of Northern Rhodesia has issued a statement about Federation which talks about the 'solid' African opposition to it. It is just not true. The local leaders of the ANC, who oppose Federation bitterly, call me 'the priest with the white collar and the black heart' because I frequently try to expose the dishonesty of some of their statements, such as that Federation will mean that Chiefs will lose their power and that the Africans will be driven out of their own land." *April 1953*

Problems of handing over responsibilities

"I have just had two days of Quarterly Meetings. Two days in which I have tried to sit back and understand what it will mean to give responsibility to the Africans, but years of subservience have so conditioned them that they will not, I almost say cannot, take over. Even when we have admitted all our mistakes and humbled our Western pride, I am still faced with the horrible dilemma of knowing that, unless I take the lead in certain ways, nothing at all will be done. I sometimes feel tempted to say to our African church leaders, 'Here, take the wheel, drive us into the ditch, it's the only way you will ever learn'. But I feel that there should be some way of teaching them to drive without smashing the car."

"Sam Luwisha has been appointed a Provincial Councillor, quite an important post in local government. Rodwell Pali was home on a week's leave from the Agricultural Training School. He is full of new ideas about better farming methods, and I am hoping he will take full responsibility for the farm work here when I go on furlough. It is strange that I, who am by nature so happy-go-lucky, find myself so often in the role of the martinet insisting on more discipline and efficiency. There is not one member of the staff here who will see a job that needs doing and get on with it. Sometimes, when I get weary of driving them on, I close my eyes for a while, in forgetfulness, but it never pays in the long run." *May and October 1953*

New arrivals know it all already

"Last week I had a trip to Lusaka in the District Commissioner's five-ton lorry and another trip into the Sala country by cycle to visit the schools. I met a very green and critical young Education Officer recently out from England, inspecting the schools. I find it goes hard with me, after working

so long to get the co-operation of the Chiefs, the people and the administration to run a village school on a shoestring budget, then to be told by a
greenhorn, 'The trouble with you missionaries and your schools is that too
many people are trying to run them at the same time.' I try hard to remember that it was not so long ago that I was a greenhorn myself." *April 1954*

The end of our time at Nambala now seems inevitable

"Mr. Nightingale is most anxious for me to continue in rural work, but
I don't see how it can be done when all the children reach school age.
Every time I walk over the farm or lean over the fence of the cattle kraal,
I wonder how I shall ever manage to work in town. I do not want to be
minister to a white congregation and leave the 'African work' to an African
minister." *October 1953*

My mental adjustments as I prepare to leave

"Here in Lusaka, where I have been for a week, I am living in such a different world from Nambala that I wonder if I am the same person. We had
a good journey into town on Thursday, just making it even though the
Vanguard car is feeling its age and will have to go into dock for extensive
repairs. I took the morning service here for Nightingale, all fitted out in
gown and bands. People liked my sermon because it lasted only eleven
minutes. They usually get thirty minutes from Mr. Nightingale.

"It looks as if the way is opening up for me to come back to Lusaka
after furlough, to take over from Mr. Shaw, the General Secretary of the
United Society for Christian Literature (USCL) when he retires in 1956.
There are tremendous opportunities for Christian literature work in this
country. I shall still be a member of the Synod and will be preaching a lot
in the Lusaka circuit. If I have got to leave the bush work and live in the
towns, my job in the USCL will take me back into the rural areas of the
whole country. My one fear is that it is too much in line with my present
inclinations! However I took comfort from the words of the Covenant
Service this morning:

> "Christ has many services to be done; some are easy, others are diffi-
> cult; some are suitable to our natural inclination and material interests,
> others are contrary to both."

January 1954

Africans threaten strike action

"There is a threatened general strike of all Africans on Monday, but I don't think it will come off. I am afraid I have no sympathy with the impossible way some of the African leaders are using strike action—it can only do their cause harm. The really big battle is coming on the mines. We have heard tonight that the European Mineworkers' Union have turned down the Foster Report on African advancement. If the Africans go on strike on this issue I am with them all the way." *October 1954*

The way ahead seems clearer

"At last the rains have come, the days are cool and the air is clear. After months of heat and dust, all the trees have been washed and everywhere new green grass is springing. I spent one day ploughing using our new Land-Rover. To watch the soft brown earth spilling away from the plough-share stirs something in my blood which is quite impossible to explain.

"It seems as though God has been waiting and chose this time to work the same miracle in our spirits. Audrey and I have quite suddenly been given new understanding and a marvellous awareness of God's loving care. We know that such blessing could come from nowhere else but God, and must be an overflowing of all the prayers that those who love us have offered up. Everything we ever believed in is twice as true, and Grace is an even deeper mystery." *October 1954*

Town and Politics

In 1955 I left Nambala mission and we went on furlough. The next year I was appointed General Secretary of the United Society for Christian Literature in Northern Rhodesia. My brief was to travel the length and breadth of the country—twice the size of Britain—with a Land-Rover book-van.

For the first year we were based at Kitwe on the Copperbelt, where I was confronted with the worst of white racism. Most of the white men who worked the copper mines had come from the Republic of South Africa, and they brought with them the doctrine of *apartheid* or 'separate development', which was applied even more rigorously here than in Johannesburg or Capetown.

The children attended a school for white boys and girls only; Audrey went shopping in stores which had separate counters for whites and blacks. The bread, tea, milk and sugar were all the same. The money was the same money for all, but black and white never talked to each other. When the circus came to town, all the ring-side seats were reserved for whites while the blacks stood in a separate enclosure at the back. On Sundays all the Christians worshipped the same God, sang the same hymns, and read the same Bible, but each race prayed in its own language, in its own church.

When a fellow black Christian travelled with me in the Landrover and I stopped for a cup of tea and a plate of fish and chips at Broken Hill, I could not invite him in to share the meal with me. The proprietor would simply refuse to serve him, not even allowing him to have a cup of tea outside on the verandah lest he 'contaminate' the cups which were kept for the use of Europeans only. It was all so stupid, so unnecessary, and I knew it was wrong.

Kenneth Kaunda

In 1958 we moved to Lusaka, with two colleagues who ran the Lusaka Bookshop, while I travelled all over the country with my Land-Rover book-van. Once a week, when I was at home, I ran a Bible study in my house for young members of the Lusaka Methodist congregation.

I invited a young man by the name of Kenneth Kaunda to attend the group at our house. At that time not many Africans entered European homes, but to my surprise he came. A couple of months previously, Kaunda had emerged from a spell of 'rustication' (expulsion by government order to a remote rural area) in Kabompo, a small town 300 miles away from Lusaka in the North Western province.

Born in 1924, Kenneth Kaunda grew up on Lubwa mission station, the only Church of Scotland mission in Northern Rhodesia. His father, David Kaunda, had come from Nyasaland to spread the Gospel among the Ba-Bemba. His mother was matron of the girl's boarding school and a teacher. She had the reputation of being kind-hearted, a strict disciplinarian, and a deeply religious woman who herself conducted family prayers night and morning.

By 1938 Kaunda had reached Standard 6, the top class in the school. He was remembered as the brightest boy in the class and a natural leader of his age group. He was as active outside the classroom as in it, a keen footballer and boy scout. He trained as a teacher while continuing his studies, and when the Munali secondary school opened in Lusaka he was accepted for Standard 7 and 8.

A young man of 22 with the highest educational qualifications any African could obtain in Northern Rhodesia, and with a teaching certificate, Kaunda returned to Lubwa as headmaster of the boys' boarding school. The position carried with it considerable responsibilities for so young a man. It also required the qualities of tact and forbearance, for all the other members of staff were older than he.

After no more than a year or two at Lubwa, Kaunda had decided that it was time for him to gain a wider experience of life. He travelled to the Copperbelt and for a few months worked as a welfare assistant in the Nchanga mine, before returning to teaching. He regarded 1947 as the most crucial year in his life. For the first time he felt the full shock of the Colour Bar, and began to rub against Europeans who spoke to him not as a fellow human being but as a lesser breed. He became a member of the local Welfare Association, and for the first time heard his own people talking politics seriously.

Kaunda was one of the first to join the ANC when it was formed in 1948, and very soon he found that political activity absorbed all his spare time and thought. He decided to resign from teaching and return to his home, where he hoped to set up in business and carry on with his political activity.

He went back to his mother's farm near Lubwa and began trading in second-hand clothes which at that time could be bought cheaply in the Belgian Congo. He would cycle the 300 miles to the Congo border, buy the bales of old clothes, consign them on road transport, then hurry back on his bicycle to Lubwa to be in time to offload them there. His ability to cycle long distances without seeming to tire stood him in good stead when he came to organise the Congress branches scattered over the length and breadth of the Northern Province, an area half as big as England.

During this period he came into conflict with the missionaries at his old station of Lubwa over the concept of Federation. In an open letter to the missionary in charge of Lubwa dated 25 March 1952, he quoted from Bernard Shaw's *Man of Destiny*:

> "When the Englishman wants a new market for his adulterated Manchester goods he sends a missionary to teach the natives the Gospel of peace. The natives kill the missionary, he flies to arms in defence of Christianity, fights for it, conquers for it, and takes the market as a reward from heaven."
>
> If you missionaries intend being of service to the British Government in the way described by Shaw you have come at a wrong time. Our forefathers killed no Europeans in this Protectorate, and we are going to make sure we kill no European missionary or otherwise for political reasons – nay we will not – Reverend Sirs. Preach how you may, we shall struggle for our Nation's survival within the British scope of struggling. We are not struggling against the British Government but against the Federal case.

In 1953 Kaunda was appointed General Secretary of the ANC, and for the next six years he was the organising brain behind its administration. As a protest against the Colour Bar in shops, he organised the boycott of the butcheries where African women were forced to wait in long queues at a hole in the wall while European customers were served as they came in at the counter. The sight of women being arrested for taking part in the boycott led him to take a vow that he would never eat meat again.

In 1955 Kaunda, along with the Congress's President Harry Nkumbula, served a prison sentence for having in his possession a number of publications that government had declared to be prohibited reading. Among them were several books supplied to him by a prominent Asian business man on the subject of Gandhi's campaign of non-violence. These wider influences were combining with his deeply Christian family background to develop a non-violent political credo.

Kaunda's first experience of travel overseas came in 1957 when he went to London to attend a Labour Party Commonwealth Conference. He spoke to a group of students at Oxford, one of whom writing to his father in Northern Rhodesia, said, "How is it that this quiet-spoken and reasonable man is regarded as an extremist in Africa?" On his return the 'African Times' began to build him up as a potential rival to Nkumbula as the ANC President, but he replied by making a public statement that he had no desire whatsoever to oust his old leader.

Raising funds for a UNIP Land-Rover

Gradually Kaunda and I came to know each other. By this time he had left the ANC and formed the United National Independence Party (UNIP). On one of his visits to my home he told me that as general secretary he was having a hard time organising UNIP, because he had no transport.

"No transport," I said, "And you think you can organise your Party in a country twice the size of England? You must be joking. How in fact do you get around at present?"

"On a bicycle," he said, "and buses and the train, which takes two days to travel from north to south, and if I am lucky I may get a lift with one of my friends for the 200 miles from here to the Copperbelt."

"You obviously need a car," I said.

"And where do you think I can get money for a car? I am broke and the Party is broke."

Rashly I said, "I will give you a car. I have a practically new long-wheelbase Land-Rover fitted with an extra fuel tank giving a range of about 400 miles. It is eighteen months old, and has done about 15,000 miles. For reasons connected with my work, I have permission to sell it. If you come around to the bookshop in Cairo Road tomorrow you can drive it away."

My problem now was how to raise the £700 I needed to buy the vehicle from the USCL. The bookshop manager said he would give me three months to find the money. Such was my enthusiasm for Kaunda, this man of conviction and charm, that I thought all I had to do was put an advertisement in the *Times of Zambia,* and all Kaunda's friends would rush to contribute.

I went to see my good friend Dick Hall, the editor of the *Times*, who fully supported Kaunda but was less than enthusiastic about an advert. So I started to walk round all the Indian shops in town asking for contributions. I thought that the Indian community, always wanting to hedge their bets, would support the Federal Party with their left hand and the African Nationalists with their right.

I was wrong. After six weeks I had raised £30. There followed many sleepless nights. There was nothing for it but to go back to the bookshop manager with my tail between my legs, and admit total failure. How he would ever manage to retrieve the Land-Rover from UNIP, with which he had no sympathy, I hardly dared to think.

Then something strange happened. I was sitting gloomily at my desk at the bookshop when an acquaintance of mine, Hans Noak, a Quaker, walked in and without a word counted out 700 one-pound notes and laid them on my desk. Before I could question him about the origin of this miraculous treasure trove, he said, "Ask no questions and I will tell no lies." I was so overcome with gratitude, I said nothing; I knew at last I would have the bookshop manager off my back.

It was not until twelve years later, long after Independence, that I discovered where that £700 came from. One day I received a call from State House. Kenneth Kaunda, now President of the Republic of Zambia, requested the company of myself and my wife to meet Sir Ronald Prain, the Managing Director of the Rhodesian Selection Trust. While we waited for the dessert, Sir Ronald said, "Five years before Independence, when His Excellency was regarded by most members of the European community as a loud-mouthed upstart politician, I had a hunch that they might be wrong. So I employed Hans Noak as a kind of undercover agent, to infiltrate both the African National Congress and the United National Independence Party, and keep me informed of what was going on. He told me all about you and your hopelessly irrational decision to supply the Party with a Land-Rover."

Our host Kaunda was enjoying the story immensely and said, "We came to call that Land-Rover 'Mother UNIP'. It only ever had one African driver, and it covered 300,000 miles. I cannot remember how many times he stripped down the engine by the roadside, but he never failed to get me to my meetings on time. We have now decided to put it on a plinth outside my little two-roomed house in Chilenje."

My growing support for UNIP

My white colleagues shook their heads in disapproval when they saw a fellow-missionary getting mixed up in politics, which they regarded as a dirty and inevitably violent game. However, for me the issue had become crystal clear. The struggle for power between black and white had begun. The only question was whether whites could be persuaded to hand over their power without the threat of violence. Kaunda, who had been deeply influenced by the teachings of Mahatma Gandhi, announced a campaign of non-violence to achieve independence for his people. I said I would join him in the campaign because I too believed that non-violent direct action was right, and I would do my best as a white man to persuade the British government that the time had come to give parity to blacks in the legislative council, in preparation for the day when they would achieve complete independence.

From the beginning I had promised Kaunda that as long as UNIP's campaign for independence remained non-violent, I would back him all the way. I abridged a little book by Richard Gregg called *The Power of Non-Violence* with a foreword by Martin Luther King Jr. The Joseph Rowntree Trust gave me money to get it published, and with a £200 grant from the Mindolo Ecumenical Foundation, I arranged to have translations made into Ci-Bemba and Ci-Nyanja.

In the early 1960s Kaunda was a complete riddle to both black and white. In the extreme European view he could be compared to a black mamba, the most deadly of snakes, whereas to moderate Europeans he was seen as an ambitious politician lusting for personal power, who should wait patiently for Northern Rhodesia to grow to full political maturity. For many Africans he was seen as 'The Lion of the North', a political African Gandhi of the unborn state of Zambia.

Black Government?

At this point I knew I had to write a book. After all, I was the General Secretary of the USCL, which had a duty not only to distribute books, but to publish them as well. I was tired of being told by my fellow-missionaries that politics is a dirty game, and that no Christian minister should get mixed up in it. I had even been told by the missionary minister of the Trinity Methodist Church in Lusaka, that it would be unwise for me to preach any more to his entirely white congregation. The whole political situation was deteriorating fast. For the sake of the white population of Northern Rhodesia I had to publish quickly.

I decided I would bring together my two closest friends, Kenneth Kaunda and Colin Morris,[1] for one day and, under my chairmanship, the black politician and the Christian minister would meet and talk about the only thing that mattered to us all: what was our attitude to the burning issue of our day—independence from colonial rule? I even knew the title of the book. I would call it *Black Government!*

A publishing challenge

To get the book written, one of Colin Morris's friends on the Copperbelt arranged to lend us their home for one day from 8 am to 4 pm, and a shorthand typist agreed to record the conversation. Generating the source material was the easy part. Getting this document into a reasonably presentable manuscript proved to be a great deal more difficult than I had imagined. First my typist allowed her husband, who was a high-ranking civil servant, to read the manuscript. He pronounced it extremely seditious and asked her to resign from the job she was doing.

We finally got it to the Rhodesian Printers Limited, in Ndola on the Copperbelt, but the head printer refused to set the type unless we were prepared to change the cover. *Black Government!* was to have a photograph of Kaunda on the front cover and of Colin Morris on the back. In much distress I rang Colin and we decided on a compromise. The front cover would have on the red background a large white question mark, and round the edge in small print would be printed *Black Government?* The back cover was to be left blank. I do not think that the African population knew the

---

1 Since his return from Zambia, Colin Morris has been President of the Methodist Conference, and successively Head of Religious Broadcasting at the BBC, and its Controller in Northern Ireland. He is an active author and broadcaster.

difference between an exclamation mark and a question mark, but the printer was satisfied and agreed in the end to set the type.

Who knows what influence *Black Government?* had on the African population? But the books 'sold' like hot cakes. I used the nationwide army of distributors of the African Mail newspaper, sending each five copies on credit. They never paid up, and in the end the USCL had to write off the money as a bad debt. I hope they felt it was their contribution to the success of the Independence movement.

Colin Morris, Merfyn, and Kenneth Kaunda, working on the **Black Government?** *book. Colin points out that "the photo was ... published in the Northern News. The motive wasn't to flatter us but to show the scandal of two white missionaries being friendly to a black terrorist."*

At that time I was Editor of the Christian Council Newsletter, which meant that I could pin a little label on my lapel which simply said *Press*. I heard that UNIP was to hold a meeting in the Askari Hall near the barracks in Burma Road. The Hall was packed and my *Press* label took me to the very heart of UNIP. I was the only white man present. I had expected to hear a ranting Nationalist making absurd claims for "independence now" or "immediate freedom from oppressive colonial rule". I was completely wrong. All that Kaunda was asking was equality in the Legislative Council, with the Governor in the chair holding the casting vote. Not only was I wrong, but 99.9% of all Europeans in Northern Rhodesia were wrong about Kaunda. So the next day I went round to the UNIP office in Lusaka, and told Kaunda that I wanted to join his Party. He said that three other Europeans had asked to join, but he thought it unwise to make our names known publicly, because of the possible repercussions on our families. He promised to keep my membership card locked up in the UNIP safe.

I declare my support for UNIP

But it was not long before I felt that I had to declare my support for the National cause. One afternoon I drove down the dusty road to UNIP's office behind the Askari hall. I said to the man in charge, "Please tell Mr Kaunda that I want my name to come out of the office safe. I want him to give me the chance to go public."

I waited for a few days, then received a message that on the following Sunday afternoon, permission had been granted by the police for a large meeting to be held in the open space between Lusaka's shops and the Kabwata African township. It had been widely publicised by word of mouth amongst the population. The editor of the Sunday edition of the *Salisbury Herald*, a paper which was widely read by most Europeans in the north, had been informed.

Sunday came but I did not go to church; instead I went down the hill to the suburb of Kabwata. On one side of the open space was a large 'anthill'. Steps had been hacked in the solid grey mud, and each speaker in turn climbed up to the summit. After each speech there was wild applause from the happy crowd, and I noticed that the only way to quell the noise was for the speaker, with his right fist clenched, to shout:

"One Zambia!"

And the crowd, now a sea of waving arms with clenched fists replied:

"One Nation!"

Then three times the speaker shouted:

"Kaunda, Kaunda, Kaunda!"

And the crowd with beaming faces replied:

"Kaunda, Kaunda, Kaunda!"

My turn came to climb the anthill. I cannot remember much of what I said, but I remember pointing to the hill where the Governor lived in his big Government house and saying: "The day will come when high on that hill, where now the European population live, Zambia will have its own university."

From my position on the anthill I spotted the white policemen with their tape recorders edging nearer, and when I shouted, "No taxation without representation," they held up their microphones to catch my every word. At one point I tried to lead the crowd with a hymn from our Ci-Ila hymn book, but it was a monumental flop.

The next day the banner headline on the front page of the *Salisbury Herald* shouted: *ARM WAVING PARSON STIRS CROWD TO FURY*. I guess I had made my mark and, although I doubt if the crowds were much interested in anything I had to say, it was unusual, perhaps unique, for a white man to be seen atop an anthill with clenched fist shouting "Freedom now" or "Kaunda, Kaunda, Kaunda is our leader."

I had not been able to tell Audrey of my growing involvement with UNIP, because Kaunda had asked me not to. However, I now showed her a copy of the newspaper. She was duly shocked, but I was relieved as I no longer had to lead a double life. Once my allegiance was made public, Audrey became my most ardent supporter in the struggle for Independence.

By this time Roy Welensky, whom I had first met as a raw, young missionary in Broken Hill, had become Prime Minister of the Central African Federation. From his seat in Southern Rhodesia, he was becoming alarmed at the growing unrest amongst the African population. In the other two 'partner' states, Northern Rhodesia and Nyasaland, he saw the opposition growing. He declared a state of emergency and required all Europeans to register for what he termed 'national security'.

I regarded this as blatant intimidation of the black population, and wrote to Welensky telling him so. Meanwhile my fellow European missionaries were busy signing up for non-combatant service. When they read about this, they felt I had made a serious mistake, and one of them said to me, "If you were a pacifist as I am, you could have written and said your refusal was on 'conscientious grounds'. Then there would have been no trouble."

In fact Welensky was furious when he received my letter, and wrote to Northern Rhodesia demanding my immediate arrest. I expected to be fined, so I made sure my only property, my £400 Ford Popular car, bought to get my children to school, was put in Audrey's name. What Welensky did not know was that our Attorney-General in Northern Rhodesia was, like many of his fellow civil servants, bitterly opposed to the whole idea of the Federation. I learned later that he was also a secret UNIP sympathiser. This man put Welensky's letter safely on the bottom of his in-tray, meanwhile asking his officers to search for a loophole in the hastily-drafted legislation. They found one and wrote to the Federal authorities who could do no other than close the gap. Welensky got a resolution through the Federal parliament, but it took many months.

Our Attorney-General could eventually find no reason for further procrastination, so one day two plainclothes policemen came down to my little office behind the bookshop. They were clearly embarrassed, but told me I should put my affairs in order in preparation for my imminent arrest. I felt a little bit sorry for them, and said they had come at a bad time, as the next day I would be leaving with Kaunda and his wife to help him write his autobiography at Sir Stewart Gore-Brown's home in Shiwa Ngandu. They left and I expected to find a letter pinned to my office door when I returned in a week's time. I never knew why, but that letter was not delivered.[2]

The Mulungushi Conference

Soon after this I saw an opportunity to sell a number of copies of *Black Government?* at a big rally of UNIP supporters which Kaunda had called for three days in July 1961, at Mulungushi, a few miles south of Broken Hill. I filled the car with books, and putting on my clerical collar, mingled with the crowds. It was a Sunday, and secretly I hoped that I might be asked by the Party to conduct prayers among the leaders, but that was not to happen. However I was to witness an experience which I shall never forget.

Speaker after speaker was denouncing Macleod's new Constitution. Hatred was rising against all Europeans, and there were those who wanted to march to the Great North Road, which ran south only half a mile away, and to throw stones at every passing European car. Then Kaunda came to the hastily-raised platform of bush poles and elephant grass.

He also denounced Macleod's Constitution, calling it a 'dog's breakfast', and went on to say that he also longed for the day when his country would be free from colonial rule. However, violence against Europeans would never achieve this, and there was a better way. He went on to outline his plan for us to make our protest against the Constitution. We each would break a law non-violently and so fill the prisons. Each one of us

2 In Southern Rhodesia, Peter Mackay was charged for the same offence, convicted and served his time in gaol. However, by the time that the summons was finally prepared to be served on Merfyn, the Federation was breaking up and the arrest of a 'turbulent priest' was no longer a priority for the Salisbury regime.

would go home and break some trivial law, such as cutting down trees in a forest reserve. I decided to paint a slogan on the road outside my house, *ZAMBIA SHALL BE FREE!* However, I did not get the chance to do this because the ba-Bemba, a tribe who have always been politically active and were Northern Rhodesia's greatest fellers of forest trees, decided to take the law into their own hands. They made up their minds indeed to chop down trees in the forest reserve, but only in those areas through which the Great North trunk road travelled. They made sure the trees fell neatly across the road, making an impenetrable barrier of trunks and branches. All traffic stopped, and the police were sent to arrest the culprits who had by this time disappeared like wraiths into the deep bush.

Ruth, Patricia, Mary Jane and Robin on a break near Livingstone

This was the point when the Government panicked. They sent in troops to burn down the villages where the tree-fellers and their families lived. Now the fat was in the fire and Kaunda had to use every ounce of diplomacy to restore order. On the Copperbelt a car was stoned and its European occupants were killed, but Kaunda's policy of non-violence largely held firm.

The political situation in Northern Rhodesia was deteriorating. When the Congo went up in flames, we had seen a seemingly endless stream of European refugees, their cars piled high with possessions, fleeing south to safety. I think other Europeans were beginning to recognise how volatile the situation had become, and were beginning to fear that the same thing could happen in Northern Rhodesia.

I felt, however, that there are times when the only way to save your life is to lose it. It would mean taking not only myself but my family into the wilderness, but this was something I had to do. So I resigned my job with the USCL. Somebody else would have to travel the country selling educational books. I had no idea what I should do next, but I scribbled a note in pencil on half a sheet of paper torn from one of Ruth's exercise books and somehow got it into Kaunda's hands. I told him that the time had come for me to leave my job and commit myself to the Independence movement.

The 1962 Election

Some time in the late fifties, Northern Rhodesia was presented by the British Government's Colonial Secretary, Ian McLeod, with a new constitution which the Colonial Office hoped might bridge the growing gap between the races. It was known as the 15-15-15 constitution, and provided for an equal number of seats in Parliament to be divided between black and white: fifteen from the 'upper roll' of the register and fifteen from the 'lower roll'. However, to avoid a political impasse there would also be fifteen 'national seats' in which blacks would be given the opportunity to vote for whites and whites for blacks. How delighted Mr McLeod's officials in Whitehall must have felt, to have so easily abolished once and for all the colour bar in African politics! In these 'national' seats in each constituency, two candidates would stand, the proviso being that the winner would have an overall majority of all votes cast and also 10% of each race voting.

It was of course an absurd idea which only officials in Whitehall could have dreamed up. And so it proved to be, when the election was finally held in October 1962, under the 15-15-15 system, recently modified a little to make it more palatable to the Africans. UNIP had only a handful of European members, but the Party, after offering to pay their deposits, were able to scrape the barrel and chose a motley selection of white candidates. I can remember only a few. There was Simon Zukas, one of the first three white men to join UNIP, Laurie Escourt, a young game ranger, and of course myself, the 'maverick missionary'.

I was asked to stand for a seat on the Copperbelt, which meant leaving Lusaka and finding somewhere to stay in Luanshya. My Party gave me a large poster reading *VOTE UNIP* which I stuck on the door of my little white van. Only the missionary in Luanshya had the courage to allow me to park my car in his drive.

My political opponent was the jovial white dentist for the area, Rodney Malcolmson, and my political colleague was a mild man named Jameson

Mwinga. When evening came and the white miners had returned from work, I set out to visit them in their homes. I never had a conversation with any one of them, because as soon as I announced that I was their UNIP candidate, the door was shut firmly in my face.

The black members of UNIP's Youth Brigade went round the streets shouting my name, and some of the more intrepid ones obtained a large tin of green paint and proceeded to write my name in large green letters on the main road into town. The District Commissioner and Magistrate had little alternative but to send them to gaol. I went round to see him in his office, and was surprised to see that he was an old friend from my days in Mumbwa. He knew that as a Government servant he had to be impartial in the election, so somehow we managed to smooth things out.

When the results of the election were announced, I received 1% of the white votes and 99% of the black. My colleague Jameson Mwinga fared the same, and Rodney Malcolmson likewise received less than 10% of the black votes, so the election was declared null and void. I stood once again for a seat in Barotseland, but by this time 'the winds of change' as predicted by Harold McMillan had blown all so-called constitution-making into blessed oblivion.

Working for Kaunda

The Zambia Youth Service

THERE NOW STARTED one of the most bizarre experiences of my life. Kaunda appointed Briam Nkonde to be the Director of the Zambia Youth Service. He was the figurehead, but I was to be his deputy, in charge of administration, with four Europeans to help me.

We immediately recruited two seasoned UNIP 'freedom fighters', who toured the African townships recruiting members for the Service, making sure they were all UNIP supporters. Within a short time we had 2000 youths on the books.

Everyone who had a stake in the future of Zambia's independence wanted to be helpful. The mines offered a campsite ten miles from Kitwe in deep bush, near a small stream. A derelict farm, Mkushi, was rented and the Rhodesian Railway offered us two hundred truck tarpaulins to cover the hastily-erected shelters in the bush. An Indian trader offered to make us—at a good price—two thousand green uniforms.

I had little idea of what I was doing, and had to rely heavily on the expertise of my four lieutenants. Two came from overseas and two were recruited locally. My Uncle Will in Yorkshire got the Young Farmers' clubs near Beverley and Driffield to send us a Fordson tractor.

Two incidents remain with me from those less-than-happy days. The first was being called out early one morning, to drive down the thirty miles to Kafue to use my good offices to rescue eleven members of the Youth Service football team who were languishing there in police cells. Apparently we had sent a team to play members of the Kafue Football Club, none of whom were UNIP. They were all members of Harry Nkumbula's African National Congress and the taunting between the boys had resulted in a fight, which the UNIP team claimed to have won, but they ended up 24 hours later in custody. Of course being 'Kaunda's men' they were quickly released.

The second event was on the Copperbelt. Briam Nkonde had invited me to witness the opening of a new experimental camp where, for the first time, boys and girls were being trained together. The Director told us that Kaunda had graciously consented that the camp be called the 'Helen Kaunda' camp in memory of his mother. At great length Briam exhorted both boys and girls to behave properly as good citizens of Zambia, and finished by saying that all eyes were on this experimental camp. It was indeed a 'pilot' project. Then he got into his car and drove back to his farm outside Lusaka, leaving me to pick up the pieces. Some pieces! Everyone had the same question, "Mr Deputy Director, when do we start our training as pilots?"

Most of the young men in the Service had very little education, but as they had been told repeatedly by their leaders that the future of the nation lay in their hands, they all expected to be trained immediately as teachers, medical orderlies, clerical staff and of course pilots. I knew that for most of them their only future was to return to the land and become good farmers, which of course was the very last thing on their minds. To a man they believed that a rural life spelt poverty and urban life meant riches. It was an understandable mistake, because with all the euphoria that surrounded Zambia's declaration of independence, the gap between dream and reality had grown out of all proportion. But on 24 October, that memorable day in 1964 when at the great stadium in Lusaka the Union Jack came fluttering down and the red, green, black and orange flag of Zambia streamed out against the sky, Kaunda our new President stood at the salute as the young men and women of the Zambia Youth Service marched proudly by.

Text of a prayer tape made for the UK Methodist Church, by Merfyn Temple, October 1964, on the occasion of Zambian independence:

There is less than a week now to go before Independence Day, and Lusaka's streets are gay with bunting. Special fountains have been installed on the lawns in front of the Secretariat building, and along the Presidential route the flags of fifty nations flutter bravely in the

October breeze. Pride of place, of course, is given to our new Zambian flag, with its bold design in four colours: green for the grasslands and the forests, black for the people who will develop these great natural resources, orange for the buried wealth of the Copperbelt, red for the blood of those whose struggle won our independence. In the top right-hand corner of the flag is the soaring fish-eagle which symbolises our hopes for the future and Zambia's determination to rise above all difficulties.

Next Friday, Kenneth Kaunda will drive down Independence Avenue through the cheering crowds, in a mile-long cavalcade of cars, and in the great Independence Stadium which has been built at Matero township, 200,000 people will roar their welcome, then stand in silence while he takes the Oath of Allegiance to the new nation. In every town and in a thousand villages, people will be listening at their radio sets to hear their first President declare his loyalty and dedicate himself to the task ahead. Our little army, whose soldiers we like to think are as smart as any Brigade of Guards, will be on parade. Troupes of traditional dancers from twenty different tribes will be performing, and 500 youths of our new Zambia Youth Service in their dark green uniforms and black and scarlet caps will go marching by.

For the first time ever, this country will feel itself to be a nation. It will enter into the sort of experience which Britain has on a Coronation Day. 200,000 people, black and brown and white, will sing their new national anthem:

Stand and sing of Zambia proud and free,
land of work and joy and unity.

Next Sunday, there will be only one morning service in Lusaka, and that will be at the new Cathedral. For the first time in our history, the denominations will abandon their own services, and in an act of unity, join in a service of thanksgiving for the nation. Kenneth Kaunda, with the adulation of the crowd still ringing in his ears, will be kneeling with us in prayer, and we shall all know that this is no mere formality for him. With real humility, he will be asking for the spiritual strength to lead his nation into peace. All those who are with him in the struggle are deeply grateful to God that we have been given this man to match this hour. But sometimes it causes us to tremble, that any one man should be asked to carry such immense responsibilities and be exposed so mercilessly to all the dangers of high office. We just keep on praying.

I shall be in the Cathedral on Sunday morning, with my family sitting with our congregations from St Andrew's, St Paul's and Trinity. I shall watch the leaders of the churches walk slowly down the central aisle, the Archbishop in his mitre, and Colin Morris in his Geneva gown with preaching bands, no doubt a little bit awry. But when I close my eyes, I shall be seeing our boys in the camps at Kitwe, Solwezi and Broken Hill, and the boys on the Mkushi project, who are making a road down into the Luano valley, where Douglas Gray first pioneered the way, and left his heart.

If a thunderstorm should break while we're in church, I shall be wondering about the boys away up in the Northern Province, who are helping the Lenchina refugees to build their homes, because their only shelter at present is tarpaulins slung from bush poles. I shall be praying for young Chifunda, the camp director at Kitwe, who has in his charge 500 youths whom we swept off the Copperbelt streets less than three months ago. The only training he ever had for a task that might well daunt an army brigadier, was two years in the waste department of a bank, during which in his spare time he led one of the Copperbelt youth brigades, and then two years in jail for political agitation. His deputy in the camp is Abel Makumba, who in 1962 used to go out with the Luanshya youth wing at night to paint my name in six-foot letters on the tarmac when I stood for election in his constituency. Like most of the staff in the Zambia Youth Service, he also served his apprenticeship in prison. Such men as these are leading the nation's youth, and without our prayer they will surely fail.

But of all the faces that pass before me as I pray, there is one that haunts me even in my sleep. I know exactly the expression on his face but not the contours of it, because he has no name. He is one of the 49,000 whom we've turned away. We only write the names of those who do come in. There are 50,000 unemployed youths in our new Zambia: our only chance is to teach them a trade or get them settled on the land, and this is the task that Kenneth Kaunda has set us in the Youth Service. So far, in spite of all the sweat and tears of the past six months, we've only managed to get 1,000 into camps. That's just 1 in 50. Last week, 50 youths with their blankets and suitcases on their heads marched out the ten miles from Broken Hill to our camp, and demanded to be taken in. We had no alternative but to send them home – I mean, back where they came from, because strictly speaking they have no homes.

I wonder if you dare to pray for those 49,000 who are queueing up to come in. If you do, and your prayers mean anything at all, when you get off your knees it means helping us to find the tarpaulins, the tractors and the teachers that we must have if we're going to house, and feed, and train these youths. Unless we do take this matter to the Lord in prayer, these boys will be condemned to a life of idleness, poverty, crime and ultimate despair. Give them this day their daily bread, and lead them not into temptation, but deliver them from evil, for thine is the kingdom, the power and the glory.[1]

In the middle of the long wet rainy season of 1965, the boys, emerging daily from beneath their leaky railway tarpaulins, refused to hoe the soggy ground and demanded tractors. When I told them there would be no tractors, they blamed all their problems on 'that white man, the Deputy Director'. I got the sack and a Commission was appointed to enquire into my activities. The Commission broadened its enquiries to investigate in considerable depth what was going on in the Youth Service as a whole.

While the investigations were going on, I was given my full pay and put on indefinite leave, so I took the opportunity of going to the United Kingdom. I remember one day that two white policemen from our newly independent Zambia came to my home in the UK, and informed me that they were investigating an allegation that I had stolen two five-ton trucks from the Zambia Youth Service. I said it must be a complete fabrication trumped up by those who wanted to see me sacked. Where was the evidence, I asked? They had none. I returned to Zambia to await the decision of this Commission, still on full pay. When it finally reported, I was completely exonerated. However, it was thought inadvisable, for political reasons, for me to return to the Zambia Youth Service.

---

1 'Merfyn Temple, Prayer Tape', October 1964, Methodist Sound Archive, British Library Sound Archive, C10/34/PT23.

My appointment to the Land Settlement Board

One day I received a call from State House to say that the President had requested that I accompany him on his visit the next day to the Kasempa District.

I went to the airport and was taken to the Presidential plane, which was an old Dakota aircraft fitted out with well-upholstered single seats. The entourage consisted of about eight smartly-dressed Africans and we were shown to our isolated seats. Some minutes later Kaunda, immaculate in perfectly-pressed khaki safari suit with white cravat, boarded the plane. His secretary handed him his briefcase bulging with files, which he sat reading throughout the entire 300-mile journey to Kasempa. Apart from a smile and a greeting, the President scarcely acknowledged my presence in the plane. Throughout the journey I kept asking myself why he had asked me to join him.

The plane began to descend, and down below us we saw long lines of children, each waving their own little Zambian flag of black, red and green. After we landed and made ready to disembark, the President passed me, walking down to the plane's exit, and said, "Merfyn, I have forgotten to bring my white handkerchief." I fumbled in my pockets and thankfully found a clean linen handkerchief, which I handed to him, well aware that if he stood at the plane's door without this badge of office in his waving hand, who would know that he was His Excellency, President of the Republic of Zambia—our President?

We were met by a fleet of Land-Rovers and began our tour of the government station, visiting the school, the magistrate's court and the hospital, then on to a beautifully-prepared buffet lunch. Kaunda talked to everyone but me. Then in the afternoon, we climbed into the Land-Rovers again and all went off to a great *indaba* (meeting) of all the Chiefs of the Kasempa District. Kaunda knew that, although this North Western Province was regarded in development terms as Zambia's Cinderella Province, it was renowned for its bees and exported more honey than any other Province. He knew just how to get the Chiefs eating out of his hand.

"Honourable and distinguished Chiefs," he said, "you are the traditional leaders of our people; without you our country would fall apart. I have been told that now this Province is exporting honey and beeswax across the world. Next time you are in Lusaka, come up to State House for tea and I will give you honey on your bread from my very own beehives."

At the end of his speech he asked for questions. An old Chief stood up and said: "We are very happy to welcome you here today; you are the father of our new nation. We know that you have made plans for a big cotton plantation in my area. You have employed an Italian man to supervise our workmen and they do not like him. They say they have never worked so long for such little pay and now they have all gone on strike. What am I supposed to do?"

Kaunda stood up and said "I do sympathise with you. It is a very difficult problem that you are facing but I have good news for you. We have amongst us here today my old friend Merfyn Temple, who stood shoulder to shoulder with us in the struggle. I have appointed him to be secretary of the new Land Resettlement Board. Comrade Frank Chitambala will be the Chairman. You remember he was rusticated with me just over the river there in the Kabompo District."

In the plane on our return, I asked Kaunda for a little more information about my new job. "Go along tomorrow to see Frank at the Ministry of Rural Development," he said, "He will tell you all you want to know."

The next day I met Mr Windle, the civil servant who had been put in charge of drafting the Constitution of this Board. He showed me how to sit at my desk with an in-tray, into which you put all the files from other departments, and an out-tray into which you put your answers. "Keep the system moving, my boy," he said. "Then you will be OK."

In those chaotic days under the benevolent dictatorship of a charismatic leader, all things seemed possible. We thought that given the money and the power and plenty of bright ideas, we could develop a country from the top down. Kaunda set up a Land Resettlement Board with Frank Chitambala as its minister. Frank was a recently-reformed freedom fighter who had shown great ability in delivering passionate political speeches to large crowds from the tops of ant hills on the Copperbelt, but knew even less about land resettlement than I did.

Frank worked out for himself, with a good deal of encouragement from his 'comrades in the struggle', that there was only one way to lift the rural masses out of their poverty and stop the universal drift away from the villages into the towns. Every one of Zambia's eight provinces should have their own Rural Service Centre, where the government would provide all the facilities available in the towns: secondary schools, hospitals, modern housing with piped water, shops, and plenty of electricity to provide bright light all night long. People would leave their villages and congregate in these havens of delight. He gave instructions to all the newly-appointed African District Governors to go out with their officials into the bush in their sparkling new Land-Rovers to choose suitable sites for these centres.

As soon as news arrived in our Lusaka office that a place had been selected, Frank would order a government plane to take us out to the nearest airstrip, where we were met by the local Governor and the officers of all the departments of education, health, agriculture, local government, water affairs, public works, police, game and fisheries. We advanced in convoy along a track which had been hurriedly hacked through the bush, to a clearing in the trees to which the local chief and his followers had been summoned. The minister would make a long speech which had been written for him well in advance, and we always made sure that we had with us a broadcasting officer, so that his speech was given a prominent place in the national news bulletin that night, thus maintaining the illusion that the government of the people which had been elected by the people was indeed caring for the deepest needs of the people.

When I asked meekly whether anyone had done a water survey, I was told that the Water Affairs Department had the matter in hand. I asked where the people who moved to the Centre would live, and was told they would all be given houses such as the one that Kaunda had lived in when in Chilenje. "How would the farmers reach their fields?" I asked.

"They would have to walk or cycle to their gardens."

"And how will you stop the wild pigs from rooting up the potatoes and the monkeys from stealing the maize cobs?"

"Ah!" they said, "We Zambians are an ingenious and resourceful people. We shall quickly learn how to handle these problems."

People themselves were never asked whether they wanted to leave their villages and move away from their gardens and their grazing lands into these centres. The men who had won political independence for their country were quite sure in their own minds that they knew best what was good for their people, and they genuinely believed that the copper mines were making Zambia so rich that there was limitless money available for the government to supply anything they asked for.

The Re-Settlement Board met to receive reports of the selected sites, and it was suggested that before the Minister, its chairman, could fulfil his promises to the people, it would be necessary to do a few more surveys and planning and feasibility studies. This would require assistance from the planning officers of all the other ministries, who when requested, replied that many European technical officers had left the country at the time Zambia became independent, and very few Africans had been trained to replace them. These had more than enough work to do developing their own unrealistic projects, so they were sorry but they could not help.

Lurking in the corridors of the Ministry of Rural Development were people of many nations on the lookout for the lucrative contracts always available in such situations. Amongst them were Greeks from Doxiadis Ltd., the world-famous town and country planners. They saw no problem; they would fly out immediately all the technical experts required to survey and plan one Rural Service Centre in each of Zambia's eight Provinces. They made quick estimates of what the whole exercise would cost, demanded a substantial sum in advance and flew home to Athens. They did not tell the minister how long it would take to prepare the plans, so while he waited he found plenty of political work to fill up his time.

In the event it took Doxiadis two-and-a-half years to produce their elaborate, totally impractical and exorbitantly costly plans, none of which was ever implemented. I worked all day from my little office on the fourth floor of the Ministry of Rural Development, as part of a small team of agricultural economists, land use advisers, agronomists, statisticians and foreign experts who had been brought in to devise Zambia's five-year development plan. We were under constant pressure from our political masters to bring about an instant agrarian revolution which would transform the peasantry, who had for centuries lived more or less successfully at subsistence level, into modern cash crop farmers.

I allowed Chitambala to live with his dreams and talk about them in parliament while I got on with the work I had in mind. I surreptitiously dropped the 'Re' from 'Re-settlement' and talked only of 'settlement', which for me meant enabling rural people to 'settle down' where they were and earn a decent living from the land they already had. I took the chance to try out my model for rural development.

Agricultural expatriate teams

In the brief honeymoon after Independence Day, the Zambian government was awash with money and as Secretary of the Board all I had to do was to sign a miraculous document called a 'requisition form' which seemed to provide, within reason, almost anything I asked for. I needed to equip with caravans any team of expatriate agriculturists who offered their assistance. I chose strategic places and they came from Holland, Germany, Britain and Sweden.

I settled the Oxfam team of five and the Dutch team of six in the North Western 'Cinderella' Province. The Swedes chose their own sites but the Germans, with their reputation for thoroughness and dedication, moved in to 'save' the Ba-Tonga of the Zambezi valley. I tell the story of the Zambezi Valley Germans in Chapter 16, *Water Tales*.

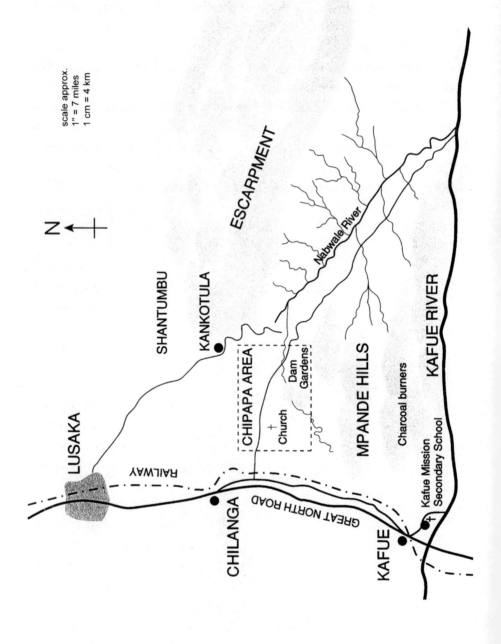

scale approx.
1" = 7 miles
1 cm = 4 km

N

LUSAKA

SHANTUMBU

KANKOTULA

ESCARPMENT

Nabwale River

RAILWAY

CHILANGA

GREAT NORTH ROAD

CHIPAPA AREA

Church

Dam Gardens

MPANDE HILLS

KAFUE

Charcoal burners

Kafue Mission
Secondary School

KAFUE RIVER

122

11 Chipapa

ONE DAY I WAS SITTING in my Lusaka house, when I received a telephone call from State House, to say that they were entertaining an eminent German professor who would like to talk to me. Kaunda had invited him to visit Zambia to advise on the question of the dispersal of industry from the towns to the rural areas. He had already advised the German government on the same issue in the Ruhr Valley after the Second World War, and Kaunda felt that new industries should be started up not only in Lusaka or on the Copperbelt, but in the far-flung rural areas.

When the professor came on the line he said, "I have been in Zambia for two weeks, and I have had the presidential plane to fly me around to wherever I wanted to go. I have visited every Province, I have had conferences and discussions with everyone from the Minister of Commerce and Industry, the Director of the Department of Agriculture to the mayors of all the major cities, but I have never actually set foot in a Zambian village, and I am leaving on the plane tomorrow for Germany. Could you possibly take me out, even if it is only for half an hour, to a typical African village?"

This was not an easy request to carry out, because there are no African villages within miles of Lusaka. The white settlers and the colonial government had taken care of that. They had made sure that all the land around the city, for at least thirty miles, had been designated 'Crown Land' and kept for occupation by white farmers only. All chiefs and their people were moved into 'Native Reserves'. However I remembered that twenty miles to the south-east of the city is a spur of land, a narrow corridor of the Soli reserve, which cuts through private farmland right up to the railway line at Chipongwe. Originally it had been designated Crown Land, but its ten thousand acres had never been taken up by any European farmer, who regarded its rocky hills and narrow valleys as totally unsuitable for agriculture. After many, many years of protest, the local District Commissioner finally persuaded the government to allow the people to return to their own land, but it needed a special order from the British Parliament to achieve this unprecedented result.[1]

I recalled that two years previously I had been asked to collect from a village called Chipapa, in this spur of land, a woman who was seriously ill and had no means of getting to hospital. Her name was Sarah Kalambalala, the wife of a retired church Evangelist who had gone to settle there. I had known her husband, Daniel, when he attended a Bible course that I had conducted at Nambala. When I eventually found the place, it came as a shock to realise how long it was since I had been in the villages. Like so many others, after early years in the bush, I had drifted into the town where one quickly forgets rural life.

What better place, I thought, to take the German professor. I might even be able to puncture some of his romantic dreams of a happy and contented people living in sweet little thatched houses with blue smoke curling into the sky, where old men smoke their pipes through the lazy day, the women dance by firelight and the night is filled with the rhythmic beat of drums and children's songs.

We arrived in the early afternoon, and the people brought a stool and a cowhide deckchair for the visitors. They sat on the ground. The conversation began slowly.

"How are you all in the village?" I asked.

"Very well, thank you, and how are you?"

"Very well, thank you," I replied, "and what are you eating here?"

"We have nothing to eat. Our stomachs are empty, there is only hunger here."

"You must have had an unlucky season," I said, "because all around you on the European farms the maize crops are looking good. What happened?"

"Oh Muluti, we are in trouble in this place. All the oxen died, so that we could not plough. When we finished ploughing, all the seed was eaten up by the partridges and white ants, and at the time of weeding, all the

1 See Chapter 12, *Shachifwa's Story*

women fell sick, so the weeds choked all the growing plants, and then we had five weeks without rain and all the plants died. When it came to harvest, all the ox-carts got broken so we could not carry the cobs to our grain bins, and the termites ate them where they lay heaped on the ground."

The village was a picture of neglect. It had not been swept for months, and piles of rubbish lay in every yard. There were gaping holes in the rotten thatch of the roofs and all the chicken houses had tumbled down. A woman came up to us carrying a bundle of rags. In it was a child too weak even to cry. It was a tiny thing of skin and bone with hollow eyes, who looked at us not sadly but with wonderment from just this side of death. Daniel had heard me call the professor by the name of 'doctor' and so he sent a message to call the woman from her house nearby. She said, "Perhaps the doctor has brought some medicine in his bag to heal the child?"

"No, he is not that kind of doctor; all he has in his bag is a camera. But what is wrong?" I asked. With one hand the woman drew aside her ragged dress revealing an abscess as big as a coffee saucer on her left breast. In her other hand she held a baby's feeding bottle with a filthy rubber teat. The bottle was half full of a grey liquid in which were floating little white lumps of un-dissolved stale milk powder.

"No, he is not that kind of doctor," I explained again. "He is not a doctor of medicine; he is a doctor of agricultural economics and planning." I suggested that perhaps she might like to come back with us in the car to the hospital in Lusaka. But the woman just wrapped up her bundle of rags and walked away to her house. She knew it was already too late, and that the time had come for her to find a quiet place, a patch of ground beneath a forest tree where she and her mother could dig a little grave, and bury their tiny child.

I climbed to the top of the little hill above the village. There I had a dream of another Chipapa, and another Daniel, and another child. Below me all along the lake shore I saw fat cattle grazing, and I heard the voices of a hundred families all busy in the fields, and there was Daniel riding home on his ox-cart, piled so high with cobs of golden maize that he didn't even bother to stop when some of them spilled off along the way. A small boy came laughing up the hill and sat down beside me on a little rock. He put his hand into my hand and as we sat there he never tried to take it away.

At that time I was living with my family in Woodlands, a leafy sub-urb of Lusaka which had been built in the days before Independence to house an ever-growing popula-tion of white civil servants, for-eign embassy staff and Lusaka's European business community. My four children had reached the limit of education that Zam-bian schools could provide, so Audrey took them to England. Since our house was too large for a single person, I decided to look for a smaller one.

Outside the family house, Lusaka

One Saturday morning in 1967, I got on my bike and rode fifteen miles down the Great North Road as far as Chilanga, then turned off the tarmac to Chipapa to visit Daniel Kalambalala, whom I had not seen since taking the German doctor to see his village. It was one of those years when the late rains fail, and as I cycled along the rutted road I saw people lining up with clay pots, buckets and plastic jerrycans to collect the daily ration of water from the drought-relief bowsers which the government had sent out to them from the Chilanga town water supply. As I arrived by Chipapa's little hill, I saw people digging for water in the cracked mud on the bottom of the dried-up dam.

When I found Daniel, he was sitting by a little fire with a group of old men squatting on low stools in the meagre shade of Shachifwa's dilapidated mud-brick house. They sucked deep draughts of acrid smoke through the long reed stems of their black clay pipes, stopping now and again to lift a glowing ember from the fire to drop it accurately in the wide-mouthed bowl of the pipe.

I joined in their grumbling conversation, and as I listened to the litany of their woes, I was moved. I remembered the dream which I had dreamed for Chipapa on the hilltop the year before. Might it one day come true? If so I wanted more than anything else to be a part of it, and to be in at the beginning of its realisation. I knew then that I must come and live in Chipapa.

Shachifwa's Story

SOME TIME ABOUT 1900, Shachifwa was born in Chipapa, a village not far off the wagon road which brought the first white traders, missionaries and prospectors from South Africa. They crossed the Zambezi at Walker's Drift and entered the country they called 'the far north'.

Shachifwa spent his childhood in the village playing with the other children and helping his mother, weeding the scattered crop of maize in the 'garden', scaring the birds off the millet and the sorghum, and watching his father's little herd of scrawny cattle. Sometimes he was taken to the Big Road to see the jolting wagons passing by. It was an impressive sight for a child: sixteen oxen, two by two, straining in their heavy wooden yokes as they dragged their wagons through rutted sand in the dry season and churning mud in the rains. In front of the team walked a young boy whom they called a *voor looper* (the dew scatterer) and behind them came the driver cracking his forty-foot whip of rawhide. Sometimes on the wooden bench up front of the wagon, there might be a *muzungu* (white man), though to the naked eye the dark tanned skin of his face and forearms would make him more brown than white.

The dream of Cecil Rhodes

Well before Shachifwa was born, Cecil Rhodes in Johannesburg had dreamed of the map of Africa painted imperial red from Cape Town to Cairo. If the dream was to come true, he would have to build a bridge across the Zambezi, and he knew that the ox-wagons of his Great North Road (still called Cairo Road where it runs as the main highway through Lusaka) would have to be replaced with a railway line. How else would the copper from the mines at Katanga in the Congo be carried south to the Cape for onward shipment to the markets of Europe, America and the Far East? How else could coal be carried from the Wankie collieries in Rhodesia to the Congo? How else would the woollen blankets and cotton cloth of the Yorkshire and Lancashire mills be brought in to exchange for the labour of workers who mined the rich ore bodies of copper which were being discovered in the north?

First train across the Victoria Falls

The railway reached the Victoria Falls in 1904. Cecil Rhodes had died in 1902, but before he died he ordered that the bridge should be built so close to the Falls that the spray would be blown over the trains, and this was indeed done. The native people who were working there prophesied that when the first train crossed the bridge it would fall off down into the river below. They watched expectantly as the first train came, and cheered when a leopard leaped in front of it, but the train never stopped. It steamed on, its cowcatcher grid catching the leopard on the shoulder and hurling it down into the seething cauldron below the falls. The white men laughed in triumph, but the people said the reason why the train had not fallen was because it had become wise and had killed the leopard as an offering to the spirit of the falls whose name was *Mosi-wa-Tunya* (the smoke that thunders), long before Livingstone named it Victoria, after his white queen.

Shachifwa, as soon as he was strong enough to wield an axe and use a pick and shovel, was recruited by Rhodesia Railways to work in one of the many labour gangs which were being employed to clear the line for the laying of the track to the north. Each man was given a weekly ration of food, and after three months of hard labour, a voucher which could be used in a white trader's store to exchange for a blanket or a length of blue cotton cloth to take home to his wife, or a cast iron cooking pot, candles, matches, soap, combs and mirrors.

At that time the North Western Territory of Rhodesia was administered by the officials of the British South Africa Chartered Company (BSAC), to which Paramount Chief Lewanika had ceded all mineral and trading rights over an area almost twice the size of Great Britain. The BSAC needed money to pay their administrators and the police force which was required to maintain the law and order needed if they were to trade in peace.

The Hut Tax

This revenue could be obtained from mining royalties, sale of land, custom duties, postal charges, and other sources. However, these sources did not bring in enough money. The obvious answer was taxation. The new white settlers were not taxed, but the company saw nothing wrong with taxing the black inhabitants of the land they had annexed. So in 1904 they introduced a hut tax which was levied on men and on all their wives except the first. In the early days the tax could be paid in goods such as gold, copper, ivory, livestock, cotton, coffee and salt. These goods were each given a value: for instance an ox was worth 15/-, a sheep 4/- and a chicken 3d. Later the tax could be paid only in cash, the hope being to draw the people into a cash economy. The annual tax was between 5/- and 10/- and if a man did not pay, he had to work for four months instead.

So it was that the problem of raising revenue from taxation became linked with the problem of labour. Villagers watched as all the able-bodied men packed their blanket rolls and trekked off bare-footed to the white man's mines and farms. The old men, the women and the children were left behind. They had hardly strength enough to grow food for themselves, let alone provide the corn-meal needed by the young men working underground on the Copperbelt.

Land sold to white farmers

The BSAC now faced the problem of shortage of food for the miners, and shortage of revenue from the hut tax. Then some white man in the employ of the company had a brilliant idea that he claimed would kill these two birds with a single well-aimed stone. His plan, quite breathtaking in its white colonial audacity, would have far-reaching consequences for the black owners of the land. It would change for ever the life of Shachifwa and his village of Chipapa.

Using a stick on the dry ground, he traced two long lines, each running roughly parallel to the Line of Rail, about twenty or thirty miles east and west of it. He explained how all the people living along the railway would be pushed sideways to settle as best they could, in what would be called Native Reserves. The land thus emptied of its age-old inhabitants would be demarcated in parcels measuring anything from two thousand to five thousand acres, and offered for sale at sixpence an acre to any white man who wished to apply for a farm. Some would come from Britain, but most would move up from the south. Boer farmers from the Transvaal who went north after the Anglo-Boer war would come in their ox-wagons with their cattle, their donkeys, their chickens, their ploughs and their wives and children. These Boers employed poor whites known as bywoners, who lived in mud huts and gave a third of their produce to the *baas* for whom they worked.

The BSAC would earn a pretty penny from the sale of the land, but that would be as nothing compared to the revenue that would pour into their empty coffers from the hut tax paid by thousands of new wage earners. The pioneer farmers would need great labour gangs to cut down trees to clear the land for the plough. They would draw them from the reservoirs of labour created by the establishment of the Native Reserves.

The natives would have to leave their families behind in the new villages of the Reserve and come to live in compounds on the farms in the same way as labourers in the north left their villages to work on the copper mines.

Expropriation of Chipapa's lands

In 1929 Chipapa's people were forced to join the exodus, and were pushed back into the narrow valley which runs down between the Lusaka escarpment and the Mpande hills above the Kafue Gorge. Shachifwa returned from labouring on the railway, to help his people construct new huts and clear a small patch of ground for them to plant a little sorghum and millet, and a few sweet potatoes. He worked with others cutting bush poles to construct a kraal for the headman's herd of cattle and goats, and then went off to look for work on the new farms opening up in the south. The land from which his people had been evicted was no more than small patches of fertile soil, scattered amongst the broken hill country which lies between the railway and the low line of the Mpande hills. This land was put up for sale by the BSAC, but when prospective white farmers came to see it, they took one look and turned away to find farms in less rugged country.

Slash and burn

The Chipapa people had a rough time in exile. They were ba-Sala by tribe, but the ba-Soli amongst whom they came to live resented their arrival. They did not like being forced to share their limited natural resources with people of another tribe. Water in the little stream ran almost dry in the cold season. Grazing land was insufficient, and the stony soil was so poor that the only way to get a half-decent crop of grain was to 'slash and burn' the virgin bush. This method of agriculture is quite adequate if there are only a few people and plenty of virgin land for them to move around in. When your slashed garden loses its fertility after two or three years, you can move on to slash another one, leaving your old garden in the healing hands of mother nature for thirty years or more, to regenerate the grasses, the bushes and the trees. But when there are a great number of people and not enough space for them to move around in, 'slash and burn' as a method of food production spells disaster for both the people and their land, causing massive soil depletion and erosion because there is no time to allow the natural regeneration of its fertility and structure.

It was not easy for Shachifwa to leave his wife and child in the harsh conditions of the new village. Added to all their other hardships was the presence of a pride of lions in the Mpande hills and marauding hyenas and leopards which sometimes came hunting for cattle and goats, leaping right over the fences of their kraal. There were also honey badgers and pythons, which came to kill their chickens.

But Shachifwa had no choice. He had to earn money to pay his 10/- tax and to buy things for himself and for Esther, whom he married in 1924. For a year or two he worked on the farms in the south, where in addition to maize, some of the Boer farmers were growing cotton and had found that the climate and the soil were good for growing tobacco. The woodlands which they cleared for their fields provided a seemingly limitless supply of timber to stoke the furnaces in the barns where they produced high quality flue-cured virginia tobacco, a commodity for which they could command a high price on the auction floors of Salisbury in Southern Rhodesia.

However, when his father died and he inherited a few cattle and some goats, Shachifwa returned home. His people were still angry and resentful about the way they had been pushed off their lands. They were not allowed to return to visit the graves of their ancestors, not even old Chipapa the freed slave who lay buried at the foot of the hill which bears his name. Why should they have to suffer in these harsh barren hills, when if they climbed to their tops they could look back on the old land from which they had been driven, and which had remained forgotten and unused for twenty years? No white man had ever come to make a farm, but the people were not even allowed onto the land to cut bush poles and grass for their houses, or to graze their cattle and goats amongst the thorn trees which had sprung up in the gardens where once they grew their food.

In desperation Shachifwa set off with other headmen to take their complaints to their Chief, who lived a two days' journey through the hills to the east. Chief Nkomesha heard their story in silence, then said he was powerless because although his authority extended over all the lands of ba-Soli, he could do nothing about the land which was stolen by the white people. Ever since the British Government had taken over authority from the BSAC, this land had been designated Crown Land for occupation by whites only. No black people could make farms there, although black workers could live there temporarily if employed as servants of white farmers, or as labourers in the fields or herdsmen or wagon-drivers.

The chief suggested that they should wait until the District Commissioner came on tour in the area to collect taxes and hear people's complaints. He might be able to do something, because he had the power and might go to the big white chief, the Governor, who then could take the matter to the King George whom white people regarded as Paramount Chief.

The DC who was harsh but fair

The District Commissioner at that time was an Englishman, who had a reputation as a strict disciplinarian and a harsh man who did not suffer fools gladly. If he should come unexpectedly on a prison gang of tax defaulters sitting smoking *dagga* (marijuana) in the shade of a tree when they should have been slashing the grass on the Boma lawn, he would give them a tongue-lashing as ruthless as any Boer farmer could give. He would usually include in his castigation the suggestion that if they were not prepared to work for him on the ground, they had better get up into the trees with their brothers the baboons, for that was the place where they belonged.

But his bark was worse than his bite, and he also had a reputation as a fair man who would listen to both sides of an argument and make a sensible judgement. He was not kindly, but he was just, and people respected him for that.

He heard the people's complaint. He recognised the injustice in the situation, and he started the long difficult legal process of getting the

Governor-in-Council to transfer this piece of Crown Land to the Native Reserve. After a sustained battle with the representatives of the white settlers in the council, he succeeded and in 1935 Chipapa was declared a reserve. The District Commissioner was a man of considerable fore-sight, and knew that if the return of the exiles took place without careful control, there would be endless squabbles about sharing out the land for new gardens. The population had almost doubled since they moved, so if they continued to grow their crops using the slash-and-burn method, they would quickly destroy their new habitat. The people would have to agree to make a dramatic break with their past, and accept all the disciplines and restraints imposed by the continuous growing of crops on the same land year after year with no chance of fallow. Another serious problem was lack of water, as there was no perennial stream on the western slopes of the Mpande hills.

The District Commissioner called a meeting with all heads of families to which he also invited an experienced agricultural officer. He told the people quite bluntly that the government would do three things.

1. It would help them to site a catchment dam to gather water dur-ing the rains, sufficient for their domestic needs, for watering their goats and cattle, but above all for irrigating a small area of land for growing a cash crop of vegetables.
2. It would demarcate land for making permanent gardens and appoint a resident agricultural extension officer to live in Chipapa.
3. It would build a cattle dip and appoint a veterinary assistant.

In return for this, the people must agree to give their free labour to build the earth wall of the dam, make contour ridges in their gardens to stop soil erosion, rotate their maize crop with a legume like beans or sunn hemp, and most of all cart the manure from their cattle kraals and spread it on their gardens.

Return to Chipapa

For a people who had never become accustomed to long periods of hard sustained labour it was a huge undertaking, but in the end the dam was built. New houses and cattle kraals were constructed; new gardens were cleared by felling thirty-foot thorn trees and then digging out their deep roots; crop lands were contoured. On the land set aside for irrigation, four families began to learn how to grow vegetables in the dry season and form a co-operative to market them in the town fifteen miles away. They were paid no wages for all their unremitting labour, and it is not surprising that the young able-bodied men preferred to leave the monotony of the village for the bright lights of the town. It was not too difficult in those days to get a town job as a garden boy, kitchen boy or office orderly making cups of tea on demand for ministers, permanent secretaries, under-secretaries, assistant secretaries, clerical officers, assistant clerical officers, and of course themselves. Shachifwa had a son called Daniel who never had the chance to go to school, simply because there was no school in his village. He grew up with the other village boys, herding the cattle and helping sometimes in the maize gardens with the hoeing, planting, weeding and harvest. But many days passed when there was little else to do but talk and learn how to beat a drum, and dance and sing at funeral wakes and watch his father Shachifwa make prayers at the graves of his ancestors.

The conversion of Daniel

Then one day a missionary came and Daniel was persuaded that he must give up his old 'sinful' ways, be converted and become a Christian. He was not alone in being profoundly influenced by the preaching that he heard. Shachifwa said he was too old to change, but amazingly Daniel taught himself to read the Bible, and it was not long before he began to preach himself. Indeed he became so enthusiastic in his new faith that he wanted to do nothing else. The missionaries, always on the look-out for dedicated young men to spread the Word and teach the catechism to new converts, were impressed. Daniel's life was exemplary, he had given up drinking and when he went to funerals it was not to dance but to sing Christian hymns and to pray.

The African missionary church grew through the work of the young men who were trained as teacher-evangelists. They taught in their village schools during the week and went out to preach in the surrounding villages on Sunday. But as the schools developed, the teachers found the demands of the children's education to be so great that they had neither the time nor the inclination to be evangelists.

The missionaries also found themselves giving more time to education and less to evangelism, so reluctantly, and as a temporary measure, they began to employ local village evangelists. Daniel was chosen to be one of them, and after a period of training in Bible teaching and church doctrine, he was delighted to be paid a small monthly wage and to be given a house on the mission station to do the only thing he wanted to do: gather little groups of Christians in the surrounding villages to preach to them, and sing and pray. He married a local girl who was baptised as Sarah, and they had a daughter whom they called Janala and a son Chipo, meaning 'gift from God'.

13 *Village Life*

As I cycled back to Lusaka from Chipapa, I realised that I needed to find out whether I could use the bicycle to commute to work. It took me two-and-a-quarter hours to get there in the morning, and two-and-a-half back in the evening because I got caught in a rainstorm, and a lot of the way is uphill. Just one journey was enough to prove that cycling might be cheap, but it was too wasteful of time and energy. I soon changed to using the little 'sit-up-and-beg' Ford Popular, which we had bought new for £400 in 1960 to ferry the children to morning lessons and afternoon games in their Lusaka schools. The car had a high clearance and would take in its bone-shaking stride the deep ruts and potholes of the Chipapa road. The journey should not take much more than forty-five minutes each way, so until I could afford a bigger car I would make do with the Popular, which by reason of its colour we affectionately called 'the coffee pot'.

The following Saturday I borrowed a small caravan from a friend in Lusaka, and we towed it down to the village, where Daniel and Sarah invited me to park it under the fig tree between their house and Shachifwa's, just near the spot where we had sat with the German professor. When evening came, Sarah knocked on the caravan door and said, "Muluti, your bath is ready. I have put it in our house because I have seen that the door of your house is too narrow for our tin bath." She had lit a candle for me, but she need not have done so, because there was plenty of moonlight coming though the holes in the roof. When I was dry and dressed again, Sarah brought my evening meal to the caravan door. It consisted of a small plate of mealie-meal porridge covered with an enamel bowl, on which was balanced a little saucer of chicken stew spiced with tomato and groundnuts.

When Daniel some months later built himself a new house nearer to the dam, he invited me to move my caravan to be with him. By then I had begun to find my caravan a fairly unsuitable place to live in. It was made of aluminium, which turned it into an oven on a hot day, and it could be cold at night. I had designed a thatched roof to go over it, supported on tall gum poles, which I made big enough to include under its shade a veranda, a bathroom and a small kitchen. Then I thought that if Daniel could build himself a mud-brick house, why shouldn't I have one too? Anyway the owner of the caravan was pressing for its return.

When the time came for me to go on leave to see my family in England, I gave Daniel £50 to build me a house on the sloping ground above his chicken run and grain bin. He made the sun-dried bricks himself, bought a metal door frame and window frame in Lusaka, and paid a local man to build the walls. He went out to the Mpande Hills to cut poles and bark string to bind the roof trusses, and Sarah went out with the village women to cut bundles of thatching grass.

I take a break in England and fast for world poverty

The Rev. Merfyn Temple about to enter Westminster Abbey to begin his fast on Monday

While this was going on, I went to England in 1968 for the World Poverty Campaign of the British Council of Churches. I have always been deeply grateful to President Kaunda for the way he backed me up during that difficult year, especially for the letter he sent me when I committed myself to fasting for nine days by Dr. Livingstone's tomb in Westminster Abbey. I do not know how many people in Britain understood what I was trying to say at that time, which was that the church has no right to hoard its silver chalices and gold-plated investments in a world where children die of hunger. In the end the message fell on deaf ears, but

137

Kaunda understood, perhaps because he knew what it was like to have been poor and hungry.

When I returned to Chipapa some months later, there was a beautiful two-roomed house measuring inside 12ft. x 10ft., a palace for a king. So began the period in my life when I commuted from village to town Mondays to Fridays, leaving home at 6.30 a.m. and returning at 6 p.m. I spent the evenings, weekends and national holidays testing out in practice the theories of rural development expounded by experts in the offices of government ministries.

The Green Revolution

This was the era of the great Green Revolution and the American Hunger Project, which promised that all the hungry people of the world would be fed by the year 2000. Along with all my colleagues in the Ministry of Rural Development, I was persuaded to believe that by using hybrid seeds and chemical fertilizers, food crops could be made to grow up to six times the yield previously obtained by traditional farming methods.

I persuaded Daniel to plough two acres of his four-acre plot of land in Chipapa, and I lent him money for hybrid seed and chemical fertilizer. We had good rains that year and every maize plant shot up to seven feet tall, each one with at least two cobs as thick as a man's wrist. No one in all the villages around had ever seen anything like it. They came and stood in wonder at the power of white man's magic (the name they gave to the white powder we sprinkled over the ground was *musamu* or 'medicine').

Four hundred miles away in the North Western Province where I was running an agricultural project with British and Dutch volunteers, they heard about Daniel's maize garden, and Chief Kasempa with his councillors came all the way by Land-Rover to witness this miracle.

President Kaunda visits Chipapa

Word got through to the President in State House of the poor villager who had been hard pressed to feed his own family, but now in one season had a crop that would give him enough surplus maize for sale to pay off his loan and bury a wad of bank notes in a tin box in the mud floor of his house. There would be more than enough to supply all his family needs for over a year.

With President Kaunda on his helicopter visit to Chipapa to see Daniel's wonder crop of maize. With him is Matthew Ndunda, Merfyn's colleague at the Land Settlement Board

Parts of our road had been washed away in the heavy rains, and though passable in my 'coffee pot' car were not negotiable by the presidential Mercedes-Benz, so Kaunda, who wanted his whole government to know that the day of Zambia's prosperity had dawned, ordered two army helicopters to transport them to Chipapa.

We were given only three days to make frantic preparations for the presidential visit, but in reality there was not much we could do but sweep up the rotting fruit and dead leaves beneath the great spreading fig tree down by the lake in preparation for the presidential *indaba*.

On the appointed day a despatch rider came with a message from State House to the school headmaster, giving orders to the children to run into their classrooms when they saw the helicopters in the sky, because the school football field had been chosen for the landing pad. When they arrived in a cloud of red dust, we saw that Kaunda had been as good as his word. Not only had he brought the Ministers of Agriculture, Natural Resources, Rural Development and Local Government, but also the Ministers of Education, Economic and Social Development, the Chief of Police, the Director of the Prison Services and the Commander of the Zambia National Youth Service.

Daniel led them proudly through his forest of towering maize stalks. They felt the weight and thickness of the cobs and wished the managers on their own private farms would do as well as this. At the *indaba* the President praised Daniel for all his hard work (quite forgetting Sarah and Janala who had done all the planting and weeding and spreading of the fertilizer). Knowing that his speech would be broadcast in full on local radio, he called on all village farmers to follow this poor man's example and by so doing eradicate the threat of hunger from the land.

The next year the people of Chipapa set up their own Productivity Council. Each of the hundred members borrowed money from the Land Bank to purchase hybrid seed and fertilizer. Unfortunately the rains failed in mid-season, the standing maize withered before producing any cobs, and everyone ended up in debt.

The Women's Poultry Co-op

Meanwhile with help from the government poultry officer in Mazabuka, Sarah with thirteen other women started a poultry club. They worked in pairs, each couple agreeing to look after a little flock of broiler chickens and Emden geese and Khaki Campbell ducks, for one day in the week. Fortunately two women in the co-op were members of the Seventh Day Adventist church who worship on Saturdays, so they did their stint on Sundays when the others went to church.

None of the women nor I had any experience of looking after day-old chicks but the man at the hatchery in Mazabuka showed us how to brood them in a box with a paraffin lantern to keep them warm at night. The baby chickens were no problem, but we nearly lost the day-old ducklings. All went well for the first three days but on the fourth day, thinking they would enjoy it, we let them out when it was raining. They did love it, but having no mother duck to teach them otherwise, they rushed around with little beaks in the air to catch the heavy drops of rain and nearly drowned themselves. Just in time we rescued them and dried them out with the warm cuddle of our hands.

It was not long before we had a fleet of a hundred ducks cruising round the lake. They loved to dabble in the muddy margins of the dam gobbling up the water snails which harbour in their guts the dangerous bilharzia parasite. For the first time since the dam was made, it was safe for the children to swim and splash in the water.

The Young Farmers' Club

A great part of my work in the Ministry of Rural Development was to try and persuade the government that it was a waste of time and money to settle urban youths as farmers in rural areas if the young men already living in the villages were failing to earn a decent living there. I knew that the best way to influence government policy would be by practical demonstration rather than argument. So I set about recruiting some of the young men in the village to start their own Young Farmers' Club. They wanted to have a regular monthly income rather than an annual income from a seasonal crop, so they decided to try growing vegetables for sale in Lusaka. I gave them all the assistance I could, even bringing out a young man from Britain to live and work with them and teach them the basic elements of organic horticulture. However I had completely underestimated the social and economic forces with which they would have to contend, and although we made a good beginning, the project never took root. Out of the ten young men who started the club, only one remained after two years, and he ended up working for a European farmer who grew flowers for export by air to Britain.

By village standards he earned good money, but being illiterate he could not read the 'poison' label on the can of insecticide used to spray his master's roses. Not realising that the liquid should never be used on food crops he took some home with him one day to kill the corn crickets on his maize cobs. Six months later he and his wife, and two of their children, died after eating an evening meal made from the flour which she had pounded from their own poisoned cobs.

Fasting on behalf of Chipapa's people

Normally, every May when the Rains are over, the Rural Council sends a bulldozer to level out the deep ruts on the five mile road which runs from Chipapa to the Great North Road.

By late May 1969, all the tomatoes on the two acres of irrigated land below the dam were ripening fast but no bulldozer had arrived. The usual lorries which came to pick up the tomato crop could not get through, even with a bicycle it was almost impossible to negotiate the deep ruts. Our Councillor made protests but nothing happened. The people were desperate. Without money from their tomatoes the people would be bankrupt.

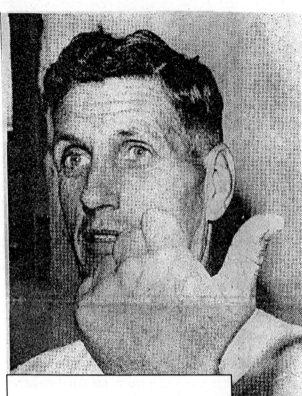

Hunger strike priest fumes over road

By Times Reporter

NOW a preacher is
hunger strike.

The Rev Merfyn Temple,
the United Church of Zam
bia, has been fasting f
seven days.

Mr Temple, a land settleme
officer, is protesting again
what he describes as t
"neglect by the authoritie
of the people of Chipap
where he now lives.

Chipapa — 18 miles sout
east of Lusaka — has
population of about 1,00
Poor roads virtually isola
it from the Capital.

Mr Temple said yesterday:
want to protest on beha
of the people of Chipap
against the bad conditio
under which they have
live. Our road is the lif
line to the hospital and
the market. Yet it is so ba
we can't get the sick
hospital.

The road, which joins th
main Lusaka-Kafue high
way, has been washe
away in parts by the rain

Flooded

There is also a stream whic
when flooded, makes
impossible for cars to dri
through. Rains have al
cleaved trenches in the du
road.

Temple can stay, says Ministry

THE MINISTRY of Rural Development yesterday put a damper on demands for the removal of Rev Merfyn Temple from his Chipapa home yesterday.

The Ministry's Permanent Secretary, Mr Andrew Kashita, said that Mr Temple was not contravening Government nor Ministry regulations through his fasting. The move could not be authorised.

Mr Temple was merely drawing the attention of the local authority concerned to the state of the road as a member of Chipapa community, he said.

The Minister of State for Central Province, Mr Moto Nkama said on Thursday he would consult the Ministry on the intended eviction of the fasting priest from Chipapa.

I went to see Dr Oliver in Lusaka to give me a medical check-up, and then announced that I was going on a fast until the road was made passable. I drank plenty of water and sometimes had a little soup. After ten days no bulldozer came, so I sent an announcement to the local Press, then went off on tour in the Kassempa District to visit the Oxfam and Dutch Rural Development teams which I had started there. I travelled with the Oxfam Director in a British High Commission Land-Rover.

After another ten days nothing happened, so on the twentieth day I went to see Dr Oliver again. He announced that I was suffering from severe malnutrition, so I went back to the Press and told them I had called off the fast. Within two days the bulldozer arrived and Chipapa's tomatoes were on sale again. Of course the Rural Council could take no action while under pressure from me, but once I had admitted defeat, Kaunda my good friend in State House waved his magic wand.

I was later to receive a rap over the knuckles from my permanent secretary, but Andrew Kashita who held a position a little higher up the Civil Service ladder, leapt to my defence.

I did not keep a diary during the years I worked first in the Zambia Youth Service and then in the Land Resettlement division of the Ministry of Rural Development but when I returned from leave in September 1969 I decided to do so. It is from that diary that I quote the following extracts, which carry the Chipapa story forward to 1974 when I finally returned to Britain.

Chipapa Diary 1

18 September: The Church and the land

YESTERDAY I ARRIVED BACK IN LUSAKA from short leave. There is bad news from Chipapa. Last night Janala, Daniel's married daughter, was waiting by the roadside for a lift when she was assaulted, robbed and left badly cut and bruised with two bones broken in her leg. It happened in broad daylight, but there were no witnesses and the police have no clues. I must get back to the village as soon as I can.

Late in the morning the Moderator of the United Church of Zambia and our local Kafue minister dropped in to see me about the problems caused by squatters moving onto the land at Kafue Mission. A number of attempts have been made to develop the land for farming, but they have not been successful. The Church now finds itself with a big secondary school, giving a high level of academic education, training boys for the 'O' level examination, and a large tract of undeveloped, agriculturally marginal land onto which squatters have begun to move. The Church knows what it would like to do, which is either to give the school an agricultural bias, getting the boys to grow their own food and so hopefully gain an interest in farming, or else to encourage settlement by young men trained at the Chipembi farm institute, to grow crops for the rapidly-expanding industrial population of Kafue town seven miles away. But knowing what it ought to do, and doing it, are worlds apart. The Church has neither the capital nor the managerial capacity to develop its own land.

Until now we have been able to put off the problem, and settle with our conscience by promising ourselves that next year we will do something about it, next year when we are a little less hard pressed for money,

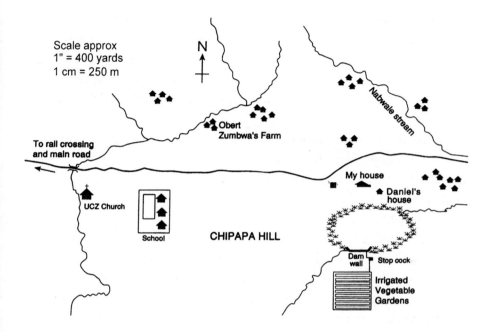

Scale approx
1" = 400 yards
1 cm = 250 m

N

To rail crossing
and main road

Obert
Zumbwa's Farm

Nabwale stream

My house

Daniel's
house

UCZ Church

School

CHIPAPA HILL

Dam
wall

Stop cock

Irrigated
Vegetable
Gardens

or staff, or time to do the thousand other things we want to do. But now we cannot put it off any longer, because since the referendum on land last June, it has become clear that our Government is going to say that the land shall belong to those who use it, and not to those who long ago were lucky enough to have the money to buy it cheap. Sometimes the Church in the past has toyed with the idea of selling some of its land, but there has always been someone to suggest that if we would hang on a little longer the price might go up.

The Moderator enquired if I knew of anyone qualified to run a farm scheme at the Mission, because he knows that I have been in England recruiting agriculturalists to come to Zambia to help us in the development of our rural areas. I am quite clear in my own mind what ought to be done, but I have no confidence that the United Church of Zambia, as presently organised, has the will-power to act creatively in a situation like this. There is hardly a secondary school in Zambia taking the issue seriously of how to give young men a vocation for the land, but Kafue could do it. All it needs is a good practical farmer to come from overseas to spend three years settling five young Secondary School leavers on five acres each just near the school. The present generation of school boys at

145

Kafue must be able to see with their own eyes some of their peers earning a decent living from the land. Only then will they believe. The capital required for establishing each settler must be kept small, otherwise the project has no relevance for the great mass of jobless school-leavers who have no other future but a life on the land. Our attempts to settle young men from the Zambia Youth Service on the land have at least driven home that lesson.

As for all the other land, I think the Moderator was faintly surprised to hear me suggest that there might be an alternative use for this valuable riverside asset. After all, there is plenty of agricultural potential around Kafue town for feeding the population there, but there is only one Kafue river-bank where the newly urbanised population can come at weekends to watch hippos and lily-trotters, to hear the song of robin chats and the call of fish eagles, to see the startling colours of malachite kingfishers and the Knysna louris which live in the tall trees by the river. Zambia spends thousands of kwachas to develop great game parks for American tourists, but hardly a penny for the recreation of the workers in the chemical factory and the cotton mill at nearby Kafue. For once let the church stop asking how it can cash in on its inherited wealth and regain the freedom to sing honestly about 'all things bright and beautiful'.

This evening I went out to Chipapa. Men have been working on the road, filling up the pot-holes and the gullies with gravel, but no trenches have been dug to take off the storm-water, so when the rain comes next month it will all wash out again. The ducks and turkeys have grown marvellously, and we have a lot more Emden geese from Mazabuka. The Harco layers are a disappointment, too finely bred I fear for the harsh conditions of the village. The warm welcome I was given by Sarah, Daniel, Chipo and the others has helped greatly to thaw an aching heart still frozen up by leaving my family in England.

19 September: Dr Fritz Schumacher visits our village

Dr Schumacher of the Intermediate Technology Development Group is here from England on a special assignment for Kenneth Kaunda. I have not met him before, but whenever I have read reports of the lectures he has given on economic development, it has set all my glory bells ringing, and his report on Tanzania last year was a masterpiece of clarity and understanding. I have always been intrigued by the fact that Schumacher, who is the British Coal Board's economic consultant, should not only concern himself with African problems, but have such a sure insight into them and some practical ideas for their solution. I was afraid he might spend all his time in Zambia meeting Government officials at top level and being taken round our show pieces of development, so I invited him to come down to Chipapa for a meal.

I took him on the regular Chipapa public tour. We looked at the ducks and the geese, and I explained how we are trying to build up our flock of Aylesburys because they are better mothers than the Khaki Campbells, and what we want is meat production because the marketing of duck eggs is such a problem. I showed him our exper-iments with inter-mediate technology pumps. We had a look at the Boys' Club's sad little garden and old Shachifwa's dying vil-lage. We went into the village shop to record the high price of a tin of pilchards and a packet of Surf. But I

Chipapa vehicle 1: the Ford Popular

could see that he was not thinking about the minutiae of our village tech-nology; he was leaving that to his secretary Mrs Porter. He was seeing the people in their poverty and wondering how they can live like that.

We went back to the house and Sarah cooked us some rice and stewed duck; unfortunately it had not stewed long enough and was rather tough. I don't think he found it very easy talking to me, because his Coal Board world seems hardly at any point to touch my peasant world of Chipapa. I was glad to have Dr. Krapf with us, the German theologian and Presi-dential Advisor on Social Policy, to be a kind of interpreter of ideas. There was no language problem; it was rather a philosophical one. I was delighted to find that Schumacher does not regard 'intermediate technol-ogy' as a kind of cause under whose banner we all must march if we are to win the war against poverty, ignorance and disease. He does not try to see it as the means by which we can stem the drift of young men to the towns, and create some idyllic kind of rural community life. He has the courage to question everything, not least our belief in the long haul, the hard slog and agony of step-by-step rural development.

"Suppose," he says, "there is some sediment of truth in what people are saying, that nothing, but nothing, is going to stop the drift to the towns, that after all there is no technological difficulty in accommodating all Zambia's five million people in three or four major population centres along the Line of Rail and on the Copperbelt. Could people really be any worse off in urban poverty than they now are in their rural poverty? Why not lash out our money on tractors and other labour-saving machines, which if people were not living in thousands of scattered villages, but in close communities, might in the end prove economic?"

Schumacher was putting up an Aunt Sally to see us knock it down, but he knows as well as we do the almost demonic power of the copper mines, which not only dominate our entire economy but which super-charge the winds of change and suck us inexorably into their dehumanising vortex. Schumacher knows that unless we find a successful means of developing the rural areas within the period of our next five-year plan, nothing can save them. They will become a wasteland abandoned by the young, where the old are left alone to die.

We were five in the tiny front room of our house, so the ten members of the Boys' Club who had joined us for supper had to sit outside. It made me uncomfortable that we could not all be together, and I know I must extend my little house with a roof made big enough to include us all. There was a brilliant moon when I went out to talk with the boys, and I knew as I spoke with them that I must not spend too much of my time living for the day when everyone in Chipapa has piped water to his house, when there is a fixed price for turkey meat, and a sure market for all our eggs, and when the fields grow soya beans as well as maize. My real job is to find a way to free Godfrey, Nathan, Zunda, Leonard and all the other young men who are growing up in Chipapa from their own Utopian dreams. It may be that their children will one day operate computers in Lusaka or plough the fields with remote-controlled tractors. I do not know, and it is not worth spending a great deal of time trying to find out. The boys have only one life in the here and now of Chipapa, and they must come to terms with it, and live it to the full, and if intermediate technology is going to help them, then we will use it. Whether these boys ever become rich and successful farmers is irrelevant; that they be free to take hold of life with both hands and enjoy living it is supremely important.

20 September: Duck eggs and Sarah's dream

After supper this evening Sarah came in for a chat. Daniel her husband left early this morning for a church meeting at Kafue Mission, to discuss arrangements for the Jubilee celebrations commemorating fifty years of missionary work in this area. I wish he would spend the time building his chicken house. He will never have it ready when the rains come.

Sarah, who is the mainstay of the Chipapa Women's Poultry Co-operative, told us of her concern about the Harco layers. From ninety-five birds we got only twenty-one eggs today. There were three dozen eggs from the Khaki Campbells, but the village people will not buy duck eggs. Somehow they have caught hold of our European prejudice against duck eggs, which is pure blind prejudice, because they are just as nutritious and no more harmful than hens' eggs, but that is the thing about prejudice: once it is there it is very hard to shift.

I wish I knew why the hens do not lay. Naturally I put it down to something wrong in the management, but the experts say it is probably poor stock. All I want is for the egg production to go up so that the Women's Co-op stops losing money, but I am not a poultry expert so I can't argue. Sarah also wanted to explain that when there is some profit she does not want it distributed at the end of the month, because the women fritter it away. It would be better to let the money

Sarah Kalambalala

accumulate for six months, because then it would seem more substantial and could be used for buying a dress, or paying for a child's school uniform. How much we need to get a thrift society started in the village, but what an uphill task it is going to be.

Sarah began to tell me about a dream she had last night which woke her up and which has been worrying her ever since. I usually feel terribly

149

embarrassed when people tell me their dreams, because I know they want me to interpret them, and that makes me feel such a fraud, but Sarah was obviously troubled and wanted to talk to someone so I let her tell me. It was quite short and simple.

She had seen two aeroplanes fly over Chipapa from east to west. The first was full of African people, and it flew over the hill and landed, and all the people got out and walked to the village. The second plane had in it a man all dressed in white. He was sitting down and she could not see his face, but when he was directly overhead, she saw floating down from the sky a cob of maize, very white, as white as finely pounded maize flour, and with the maize cob were three shelled ground nuts. She received these into her hands, and found suddenly all the other passengers from the other plane gathered round her and praying.

That was all. I asked her if she had often had this dream, but she said it was the first time, though right at the end of the dream they were all together in a great house, and she had sometimes dreamt about the same house before, and it was filled then with seats all covered in gold. I asked if she had heard anyone speak in her dream. Had she received any message? But she hadn't.

What was I to do? I have very vivid dreams myself and get a lot of fun from remembering them, even the nightmares. But for Sarah it is different. Her dream has significance. She must try to understand what it means. There are no old men left in the village whom she respects enough to go to for help, so she has turned to me. I cannot leave her alone with it, so I said I would think and pray about it and we shall together try to understand what it could mean. It is a big responsibility to interpret other people's dreams, but not one I as a Christian minister can duck. It is strangely quiet for a moonlit Saturday night. No drums are beating and no-one seems to be having a beer drink or a dance tonight.

21 September: Farmers cannot go on mining the soil

It has been a quiet Chipapa Sunday for me, with forty people in church and the preacher speaking on the parable of the sower. This afternoon Daniel came in with some money from those members of our Chipapa Productivity Council who had sold their grain after harvest. They are still all heavily in debt after the crop failure of the 1967–68 drought. They had borrowed money again in 1968–69 for the purchase of good seed and

Off to work in Chipapa's irrigated gardens

fertiliser, hoping to get enough surplus on their food crop to sell it and pay off both their debts, but the heaviest rains for ten years swamped the crops, and there was again hardly any surplus for sale after putting aside enough grain for themselves and their poultry for the coming months. We all know that the provision of seasonal credit is vital for the peasants if they are to get seed and fertiliser for the improvement of crops, but when through no fault of their own they are hit two seasons running by bad weather, it is hard for them to believe that borrowing money to improve the crop is really worth while. In the past they have ploughed and planted when the rains come, and if they have been lucky they have had enough food to eat and a little left over for sale. If they have been unlucky, they have tightened their belts and got through the hunger months by digging roots in the bush.

But that was all before they became so dependent on a cash economy. For a man so much in debt, Daniel was still hopeful. Perhaps the good Lord would give him a good season this coming year and somehow he will scrape together enough money to pay his debt, but there are some members of our Productivity Council who do not have even enough maize in their grain bins to see them through to the next harvest, and they can pay back nothing so they go deeper and deeper into debt. A great part of our problem at Chipapa is our dependence on maize. This is why

our experiments this year with soya beans and vegetables and the management of livestock are so important. The conservation of the poultry
manure would save us a lot of expenditure on chemical fertilizers. The
introduction of better seed alone will double the crop, but that would not
help to get across the fundamental lesson that we must not take out of the
ground more than we put into it.

This is a hard lesson for us to learn who live in Zambia, where for a
thousand years the people have had enough land to settle on where they
wished, to chop down trees, burn them, plant their crops, and move on to
new ground when after three or four years the old became exhausted. It
was not a dangerous way of living when land was limitless and the bush
had time to regenerate and return fertility to the soil, but those days have
gone. Now there is pressure on the land because the hoe, the plough, and
the tractor have enabled people to cultivate much larger acreages. Not
only is the land exhausted, but time is running out too. It is now too late
for an easy slow transition from the old methods to the new. There must
be an agricultural revolution, or we shall destroy the land as the Tonga are
doing in the Gwembe valley.

I disagree profoundly with those who believe that the revolution can
be achieved by the sudden introduction of mechanised agriculture, hybrid
seed and artificial fertilizers. It is not that Africans cannot be taught to
handle machines and manage farms. Of course they can, as one day they
will work and manage the copper mines. The real revolution has got to
come in the minds of the peasants themselves, an understanding that the
soil is a living thing which needs not 'medicine' (our local name for fertiliser), but what the doctors call TLC—tender loving care. But if ever
I talk like this here in the Department of Agriculture of our Ministry,
I am given my dunce's cap and put in the corner with all the other cranky
members of the 'muck and mystery' school.

22 September: Men on the Moon – Tractors

I was having my duck egg for breakfast this morning, when Chipapa's
Headman old Shachifwa, Daniel's father, came in. It was the first time that
I had seen him since getting back, because he has been over at Chipongwe
trying to run a butchery. He must be nearly eighty now, because he paid
his first poll tax in 1910. It is one of the things I like about our house at
Chipapa, that people drop in unexpectedly for a meal. He asked me what

I thought about the Americans having flown to the moon. He said he believed it because he knew that the Americans were very clever people, but there had been a great deal of discussion in the village amongst the older people who found it impossible to believe. They had two difficulties. One was that people could not walk on the moon because they would not have any sky there since they were in the sky already. The other problem was about God. God is somewhere up there in the sky because he sends rain, and nothing in the lives of the people is more important than rain. Somehow, men on the moon would interfere with God's benevolence. "Anyway," Shachifwa said, "what's the point of going there, since they found no trees to build houses with, and no grass for grazing cattle?"

The newspaper today has a front-page spread about the 'lazy and dishonest farmers' who borrow money from the Government and do not pay it back. I suppose they think that Shachifwa is one of them. In 1966 he was persuaded by an enthusiastic Credit Officer to borrow £100 with which to hire tractors. He was told that the oxen he had relied on in the past were far too slow to get the land all ploughed at the first rains. That season was the good one when Daniel grew his miracle crop using good seed and fertilizer, but after Shachifwa's land had been tractor-ploughed, he planted his usual poor seed and put on no 'medicine'. The result was that in spite of the large acreage his crop was poor and he has paid nothing off his loan.

24 September: A bush fire

I had to give a lecture on rural development at the National Institute of Public Administration. We had a very good discussion afterwards, and as I had to pick up the people who had come in to see Janala, it was nearly 8:00 by the time we got back to Chipapa. As we approached the house I saw a forest fire burning on the hill. Daniel was away and Sarah had to get supper for Chipo and Trevor, so I went out alone with the two dogs to beat it out. Fortunately the fire was backing up against the wind and I managed to get it under control before it crept over the brow of the hill, but I had exhausted nearly all my strength by the time the job was done.

3 October: Potatoes at tuppence a pound

I bought some dried fish for the boys and headed back to Chipapa. I was tired after a long hot day—we had the hottest September for seventeen years. Only three members of the Boys' Club turned up for our weekly meeting. I began to question them very closely about this and discovered that most of them have lost heart. We have reaped a fairly good potato crop, but the maximum we can get from the Marketing Board in Lusaka is 2p per pound, while the same potatoes are being sold on the streets for 5p. I can hardly blame the boys for saying that the return they get for their labour is so small that it is not worth the effort, and that there can be no future for them in small-scale farming. They see the men who are working on the road and getting 50p per day. I am told that all the club members who come from Mulendema spend their days in Peter Mbewe's Tavern. When I asked where they get the money from for the beer, I was told that they wait for people coming out of town who buy them rounds at the bar.

We are having a problem getting water onto the garden, because a grass fire burnt out a section of the plastic piping to the dam, and also destroyed a number of our tomato plants.

5 October: Do we sack drunkards?

Sunday mornings before church is our time for getting the house tidy. We are a bit cramped just now, because the chicken room and grain store is not ready. Matthew Ndunda and another local farmer Juda Kibika gave us a thousand bricks each, but we have been building for six months, and still the roof is not on. The result is that my bedroom which is 8ft by 8ft, has to be used to store the eggs and the potatoes. Anyway it is better than during the rainy season when I had to brood the day old chicks by my bedside. Their cheeping would wake me up if the hurricane lamp went out.

In church this morning we were six men, seven women and five children. Daniel preached from John 15 about The True Vine. We had a discussion after the sermon about casting away the branches of the vine which bear no fruit and pruning those which do bear fruit. We applied it to the Boys' Club, and asked ourselves whether we ought to throw out the boys who get drunk at the tavern.

Chipapa Diary 2

8 October: White man's magic

OLD MAN SHACHIFWA came with me to Lusaka this morning. On the way, we passed the house of a certain man who was notorious for his rough handling of the 'natives' and once killed a workman with his bare hands. The Old Man asked me where the Europeans got their 'medicine' from. He often talks about the European's *mana* which includes power, skill, cleverness, wisdom. Do they get it as Africans do from the bark of trees and roots? Or do they dig it out of the ground? We passed a tractor on the road and the Old Man said, "Ah, that is what makes the European farmers rich! if only I had a tractor, just to get the maize planted when the rains come, I would be rich too."

Shachifwa is old and his houses are tumbling down. He is always asking me how he can get the money to buy some sheets of corrugated iron, because he knows he soon will not have the strength to cut poles and grass for thatching.

10 October: In the darkness a candle burns

It has been a hot and messy day with nothing accomplished at the end of it. I felt disappointment and depression seeping into every corner of my being, and the more I bailed it out the more it rose, and by evening I was ready to sink. I slept through the eight o'clock news then went straight to bed. I was wakened in the small hours by the geese, but the dogs were not barking so I did not go out to investigate. I lit the candle and lay fighting the depression of the previous day. Perhaps it was the candle flame in the darkness of the room that made me think of the light that overcomes the darkness in the world. Something set me thinking about the parables of the Kingdom, the seed that grows secretly, the pearl that makes it worth while to sell everything else to get it. The Kingdom is not something far away that is for my grandchildren's children and Kaunda's grandchildren and Chipo to enter. It is here, and it is only my fault if I do not go in. I waste far too much time prising open all the wrong doors. Let's face it, the door is an open door and children can go through, no trouble at all.

11 October: A dying ox and a child with kwashiorkor

Janala has been discharged from hospital today so I went to Lusaka to fetch her. Her leg is still in plaster but she can walk with crutches.

I picked up the two policemen who guard the Chipapa grain store at night. For some reason the Police Station at Chilanga had not sent transport to collect them. One of them had been at school in Uganda. He thought it was a wonderful country where the cost of living was very much lower than Zambia. There you can buy all the bananas you can eat for 6d whereas here you can sometimes pay 6d for one single banana. "Everyone in Uganda is well educated," he said, "even the loafers in Kampala have been to secondary school!"

When I got back to Chipapa at midday, I found five of the boys sweating away trying to water the garden with buckets carried from the well. They were not using the pump which sucks water from the dam, because the fire had burnt out a section of the black plastic piping. They were waiting for a chance to go to Lusaka to get another length of piping. I quickly realised that all they needed to do was to move the pump nearer to the water and re-arrange the reticulation in the garden. It only took an hour to get it fixed up. The black piping was so hot in the sun that we had to take our shirts off to make oven cloths to hold it. What a revolution this plastic piping has made to our problems of water reticulation! A completely unskilled person like myself can do in a matter of hours what it used to take a skilled plumber days of work, cutting and threading and joining galvanized pipes.

In the evening I walked along the edge of our 'little lake', enjoying the sight of geese grazing on the bank and our flotilla of noisy ducks on the water. A boy came driving what looked like a fine healthy-looking ox, but it was actually very sick, because every now and again it would stumble and almost fall to the ground. There was something wrong with its hind-

The house in Chipapa

quarters, but I could see no lesion in the flesh. The boy said it would soon die. It is one of Kapipe's four oxen, and that will make it tough for him when we start ploughing next month.

There were women and children fishing with canes along the lake shore. They seem only to catch little ones, and are lucky if they have a small plateful at the end of the day. One of the women who comes from Taulo's place on the other side had three of her little daughters standing in the water with their fishing canes. How thankful I am that our ducks by gobbling up the snails have eradicated all danger of them being infected with bilharzia. She had another toddler and a year-old baby on the bank. The baby's hair was dusty red and I would think showing all the signs of malnutrition. I tried to explain that the child was not being properly fed, but all the woman could do was come out of the water and give it her shrivelled breast. As I talked to her wondering what I could do, I was thinking of the boy I had picked up that morning who spends £8 a month on his beer.

24 October: The new roof on my house

I started at dawn today to get a new roof put on my house at Chipapa, but first I had to clear the house of everything before we stripped off the thatch and all the rotten purlins. I had a lot of helpers, Daniel and Jackson from the village, and Leonard and Nathan from the Boys' Club.

Leonard got a fright when a small green snake came out of the thatch and wrapped itself round his neck, he pulled it away before it bit him which was lucky, since I think it was a deadly boomslang. It was one of the hottest days I have known, working up for rain, and we had to keep asking for cups of water to be handed up to us on the roof. By dusk the last nail had been hammered home, the new veranda had been added and asbestos sheets had taken the place of bundles of grass, but only just in time, for it began to pour with rain.

25 October: Fisticuffs

I went over early this morning to Jackson's house to see if he would help me with the alterations to the house, because he is about the only person in the village who knows how to use a level and lay bricks, but he was busy using the grass I had taken off my roof to thatch his grain bin. He obviously had to get his food store covered before another storm came, so there was nothing for it but to teach Nathan how to lay bricks, and even Chipo, aged eight, helped me knock down an inner wall and shovel out the rubble. Daniel was busy gathering firewood for his brick kiln, so Nathan started on the whitewash.

At about midday Godfrey, Daniel's nephew and a member of the Boys' Club, wandered over to get some medicine for a bee sting. I heard an argument begin between him and Daniel. They have always had a fairly strong antipathy to each other. Daniel thinks Godfrey is a loafer, and does his best every time they meet to persuade Godfrey that he ought to be a good boy and work hard and come to church. Godfrey thinks Daniel is an interfering old so-and-so. The argument went on and on about whether Godfrey should have been helping us with the house, and they shouted louder and louder until Daniel was saying, "Get out of my sight you lazy good-for-nothing ..." and Godfrey was saying, "I'm not going till I get back my membership ticket of the Boys' Club, because I have resigned from now on, you ..."

Then they began to fight. Daniel is a little man, but he is very tough, and when I heard Godfrey howling in pain I had to go and separate them before any serious damage was done. Nathan went on quietly with his building and Leonard with his whitewashing. It was a village scene they were all too familiar with, and their only comment was, "If I had been Godfrey I would have run a bit faster to get out of Daniel's way."

I think Daniel was a bit ashamed of what he had done, because he came and worked with me till dusk, hammering out a piece of old zinc to make a gutter for the roof.

3 November: Is all overseas aid bad?

Daniel came with me to town this morning and I left him at the mortuary, where people were gathering round the body of Herbert Shankwaya who was killed in a motor-car accident on Saturday. Daniel spent most of yesterday helping to dig the grave of a woman who died in Shincebe's village, just over on the other side of the dam. Last Wednesday he attended Chief Nkomesha's funeral. This preoccupation with the disposal of the dead is enormously time-consuming. The bigger a man's extended family and the wider the circle of his friends, the more time he must spend paying respect to the dead. I wonder how they deal with the funeral problem in Communist China. I am sure that funerals used to play a very big part in the life of the old China, but it certainly reduces the number of man-hours that can go into food production in the rural areas.

Bob Liebentall, the young economist who works down the corridor from my office in Lusaka, came in for a chat this afternoon. He has been very busy over the past few weeks working out the details of an enormous nationwide cattle scheme being sponsored by the World Bank. Bob was at Oxford under Sutcliffe and he wrote his thesis on the subject of 'Aid to Underdeveloped Countries'. He believes on the whole that all aid is totally bad, because of its effect on the recipient. In theory, when the World Bank steps in with a massive loan to put our cattle industry on its economic feet, we should in Zambia be saving money to put into another development project, which we would not have been able to undertake had it not been for the World Bank loan.

What happens of course is that we take the loan, hope we shall be able to pay the interest on it when the time comes, and immediately spend what we have 'saved' on increasing our consumption. It wouldn't matter if we spent it on more capital goods for real development, but we buy more Mercedes-Benz for more Ministers to ride around in. All too often aid is 'money given by the poor in rich countries to help the rich in poor countries'.

Not being an economist myself, I cannot really argue with Bob, and I know that he is more right than wrong and that Nyerere's economic policy in Tanzania is a great deal sounder than Kaunda's in Zambia, but this total dismissal of all 'aid', however given, as a bad thing for Africa, smacks to me of the argument that wine is bad because people get drunk and sex is wrong because people have too many babies. I cannot believe that it is totally a mistake for the rich to help the poor. Giving and receiving must somehow be conceived as a complementary thing. We have to work this thing out in Chipapa between myself the rich man and Daniel the poor man, before we have any advice to give to Oxfam, or Christian Aid, or the British Government, or Kaunda, or the boys in our Boys' Club or in the Zambia Youth Service.

Jesus did say that it is more blessed to give than to receive, and he did tell the rich young ruler to give away all that he had to the poor, so there must be a right way of giving. That might be the secret: it could be that the only kind of giving by the rich that is any good, is when they give everything. Perhaps 1% of the GNP of rich countries is quite literally worse than nothing, because it is 'the all' that they can spare and that is not 'the all' that Jesus was talking about. What is 'the all' that I have to give to Chipapa?

5 November: We must return to the land or we shall starve

I have come to the conclusion, as I did when I was trying to persuade people ten years ago to accept the inevitability of African majority rule, that when people's minds are closed, no amount of talk will open them. I can argue the case for the hoe and the ox over against the tractor at this stage of development until I am blue in the face, but I have never yet got a 'mechanisation' man to change his mind because of my arguments.

What we need is a real crisis in Zambia, economic or political, which will close the door to the import of tractors, mechanical cotton pickers, luxury cheeses and Mercedes-Benz, and make us recognise that we either return to the land or starve. Fortunately I feel no responsibility to engineer such a crisis because it will come as certainly as night follows day. I think the financial and the political crises will coincide. Tonight I read Colin Morris's book, *Unyoung, Uncoloured and Unpoor*. This is the book that will make his name and for which he will be remembered. He has faced the crucial issue of our time and spoken the prophetic word as no one else can ever again. I have now got to try and apply what Colin says—not in terms of the struggle between Kaunda and Ian Smith[1], but between the peasants in Zambia and the 'Ba-Benzi'[2], between the rural poor and the urban rich. It is a terrifying thought that violence may be the only way of righting wrong. We have however an inescapable responsibility to exhaust every other means of bringing about a change before we resort to violence. I believe the end of the road has been reached as far as Rhodesia is concerned. Ian Smith is as representative of evil as Hitler was and he should be tried for murder, but this is not the time for violence in Zambia.

6 November: We sugar the pill, but they will not swallow it

This morning I drove from the Copperbelt to Lusaka thinking all the time of Colin's book. The Jesus of history now seems much more real. The probability that the Cross was the badge of death for the Zealots does not make a lot of sense to me, but the better we understand the Jesus of history, the more relevant he becomes for our day. If we could find a way of smuggling thousands of copies of Colin's book into Rhodesia, we might get the Church there to consider the possibility of becoming the spearhead of the movement of national liberation.

This afternoon I met with officials of our Ministry and the United Nations team to consider their preliminary report on the Zambia Youth Service. It became quite clear as we talked that the situation has gone beyond the stage when it can be patched up. There must be a quite new approach of the ZYS leaders to the problems of settling youth on the land. We made polite suggestions about the need for a co-ordinating committee to relate the training programme of the ZYS to that of the Department of Agriculture. We went once again over well-trodden ground, explaining why co-operative settlements have been a failure, and we tried to sugar the pill for the Youth Service by explaining how their youth settlements were only a part of a much bigger question, but their minds are closed. For them there are but two alternatives. Either youths must go back into

1 Ian Smith declared independence unilaterally in Southern Rhodesia in 1965, setting up a white minority regime that lasted till 1980.
2 A slang and rather pejorative term to describe people notorious for a taste in luxury cars. The name sounds like an African tribe.

a primitive past, when naked savages cultivated their 'slash-and-burn' gardens with their digging sticks, or they must make the great leap forward into modernity when the farmer dons blue overalls on a weekday and rides his tractor, while on Sunday he drives to church or the local beer garden in his Mercedes-Benz. There are no intermediate stages, there is just the old and the new, the past and the future, the darkness and the light. They will not stand steadfastly in the present, proud of their own past and humbly asking questions of the future.

13 November: George Mwando's ox killed by a hyena

This morning I was listening to the BBC outline of the British Press comment on the world news when Daniel came in for a chat. His preoccupation with funerals over the last month has as usual made him fall far behind in his farming schedule. 15 November is the recommended date for the last planting of the maize crop, as the best results from maize are obtained when the plant grows during the warm days of November and December, and the cobs can fatten in the early weeks of the New Year. The yield drops rapidly as the date of planting is delayed, but Daniel has not yet started looking for his oxen, which have strayed off somewhere in the hills towards the Kafue River. He is still busy trying to get the thatch

Chipapa Vehicle 2: the vanette. The frantic activity, and the huge load on the roof, indicate the heavy demand for the use of this transport.

put on the roof of his chicken house before the heavy rains wash away the mud-brick walls. Last night a hyena killed one of George Mwando's four oxen less than half a mile from our house, and a young steer drowned in the little stream which came down in flood yesterday afternoon.

In the whole village I have seen only one man ploughing. They all know the value of early planting but *buzuba leta tunji*: tomorrow is another day. Procrastination is not the same as taking no care for the morrow. Procrastination is what you do when you have given up hope that anything can ever change. That is the basic attitude of the people in Chipapa. Anyway Kapipe is going off today to look for the lost cattle in the hills, and tomorrow Daniel's brother-in-law is coming to help with the thatching of the chicken house.

I picked up the man who used to work for us as a garden boy in Lusaka and now lives in Chipapa. He asked for a lift into town to buy a bag of hybrid maize seed. It will cost him £7.50 for a hundred pounds, which will be enough to plant five acres. I feel I ought not to be going to Nairobi for the Youth Conference on Saturday, but should be here to help the people in Chipapa get on with the planting. No one is coming to buy the chicks that the women have been brooding, and which are now inoculated against fowl pest and ready to go out to the people. It is partly our fault because we never got started on the poultry evangelism campaign in the surrounding villages. We also procrastinate.

2 December: How blessed are the poor?

This morning I was standing by the car waiting for Sarah to bring a basket of grain which she had already asked me to take up to Annie Musunsa in town, and suddenly I was aware of the beauty of the day. Five egrets appeared high above the little lake, their wings brilliant white against a dark cloud, all the leaves of the trees had been washed by the rain in the night, and the low light of the sun shone on little Trevor's bright eyes and burnished the blackness of his skin.

I had been listening last night to a talk on the wireless about what man is doing to pollute the atmosphere of our world and contaminate the water of our rivers and lakes. The man who was lecturing said, "Perhaps we should not be saying that there are too many undeveloped countries in the world, but that there are too many developed countries. It is the developed countries with their factories and their machines which are the destroyers ..."

I wonder if he is right? Could it be that encouraging the people who work the land above our lake to use artificial fertilizers in their fields, we might so increase the phosphate and nitrogen content of the water that one day the fish would die? Why did Sarah have to run after Trevor to catch him before he could get down to the lake and dress him up in his little shorts and shirt to take him to town?

> Behold the lilies of the field. They toil not, neither do they spin; yet
> Solomon in all his glory was not arrayed like one of those.

If the poor are blessed and the rich are accursed, then why do we spend so much of our effort on 'development' which in Western terms is trying to make poor people rich? I think there must be a great fallacy at the bottom of all our talk about world development. I have just been reading D. G. Arnott's review of Lester Pearson's report 'Partners in Development', and it appears that the one criterion of development is whether the annual economic growth rate of a poor country can be maintained at 6%. Zambia's growth rate is better than 6%, but over the weekend seventeen people were killed outright in Lusaka alone in motor-car accidents.

The copper mines can get richer and richer, and we can export more and more copper and import more and more Mercedes-Benz, and when Robert McNamara at the World Bank looks at the statistics he can pat us on the head and tell us to go to the top of the class, but Chipo will be a year older and the chance of him finding a job when he leaves school is that much slimmer. Surely instead of the economists rating the poor on their GNP, they should now start assessing development in terms of the DCW: 'Distribution of the Common Wealth'.

Every year a nation produces wealth by the labour of its people, and some way needs to be found for assessing the distribution of that wealth, whether it be copper bars or cabbages. The copper miner who works an eight-hour shift lashing ore underground on the Roan mine has no right to a higher wage than Daniel working for eight hours under the sun at Chipapa. But the problem is that Daniel doesn't: he digs graves and preaches at funerals, and Kapipe spends most of the week getting drunk.

Who was Jesus talking about when he said 'blessed are ye poor'? It must have been the ordinary peasant folk in the villages of Galilee. They were not unemployed, nor were they starving under-nourished children. Who were the 'rich' whom he cursed? They must have been landowners and merchants and money-lenders who had grown rich at the expense of others who worked for them.

16 Water Tales

The power of water

IN 1949 ONE OF THE OLD PIONEER MISSIONARIES wrote an article in the *Northern News* under the headline, 'Who will dare go where Dr. Livingstone failed to go?' He was referring to a gorge that lies downstream from the Kafue Training Institute, and he said that he was the only one who had ever got beyond the rapids at the entrance to it. No white man had ever been known to pass right through the gorge, and the few African fishermen who had penetrated into it from the small streams to north and south, spoke of steep cliffs, cataracts and impenetrable thickets of scrub and thorn.

It was the urge to know the unknown that led Len Matthews, the Kafue Institute's principal, and myself to decide that we would make the journey. We engaged four carriers to accompany us, but after our first night in the bush three deserted. We chose a time when the river was exceptionally low and, scrambling from boulder to boulder, round the bottom of steep cliffs and through the tangle of creepers and fallen trees, we made the journey. On two nights we could not find any patch of ground between the rocks to spread out our sleeping bags, and all our food was finished long before we emerged at the other end. Never before, or since, has it been brought home so forcibly to me that water has such power. Sometimes for half a mile through the gorge the water was white with foam, and day and night our ears were deafened with the rush and swirl of the tumbling waters. It is power running away to waste, and a hydro-electric scheme is such a beautiful and satisfactory thing, because nothing is destroyed by it. This truly is working with nature and using all man's skill to harness her latent energy. Of course the real beauty of the Kafue scheme is that once the water has rushed through those incredible tunnels and dropped hundreds of feet sheer down into the turbines at its foot, the same water can be used again and again yet lower down. How lucky we are to have been given such power in Zambia.

Water on the land

Water has the power in Zambia to release energy in another and quite different way. We all know that Zambia has immense problems with its agriculture. This is nothing to do with lack of skill or hard work on the part of our people; it has to do with the way the rains fall. Not until the month of November can we begin to get our hoes into the hard ground, and by March the land is dry again. That is only five months of rain during which to cultivate crops, and even in those months we can get a drought which will shrivel and destroy the growing crops. If you allow one month for harvesting the crops when the rains are over, that still leaves you with six months during which cultivating the soil is out of the question, and it is tough on the animals too. The cattle, which put on weight when the grass is green, have a hard job to keep alive during the latter part of the dry season when the bush grass has dried and been swept by fire. It always makes me annoyed when people from East Africa draw odious comparisons between Uganda's remarkable agricultural achievements and our own, which are so deplorable. If *we* had two rainy seasons every year it would be a very different story.

Where we *are* fortunate in Zambia is that we are richly endowed with lakes, streams and rivers. If we can once learn how to conserve our water and get it onto our lands, we shall enable our people, who normally sit partially idle for six months of the year, to work all the year round in production. Water, I am certain, is the key which can unlock Zambia's rural wealth and bring a full life to our hundreds of thousands of peasant farming families. I had known this to be true in theory, but it was not till I went to live at Chipapa that I came to believe it in my guts.

The Chipapa dam

In 1950 when the people moved back into the Chipapa area from the Mpande hills, some enlightened colonial administrator or far-sighted agricultural officer realised that the building of a dam to conserve the rainwater running off the Mpande hills would provide water to be used not only for the people and their cattle, but also for irrigation. I have never heard the name of the man who designed the dam, but whoever he was, he knew his job and the dam has stood for twenty years with no erosion of the spillway and hardly any seepage through its rammed earth core. Laid snugly in the base of the dam wall is a six-inch pipe with a valve operated by a small wheel. From there the water is carried by gravity onto an area of two acres which has been laid out for irrigation.

The irrigated gardens

When I first went to live in Chipapa, only one man and his family worked on the irrigated garden, but this year [1974] on Good Friday I counted eight spans of oxen working to plough the small plots of land between the furrows, and on Easter Monday there were over a hundred people, men and women, old and young, working in their irrigated gardens. Eighty families are kept busy during the whole of the dry season producing vegetables from this area, and there is enough water to flood each plot once a week, which is quite enough for the cabbages, beans, peas and tomatoes which grow there. Not every year has been as good as this, when the rains went on late and the dam has filled right up to the top of the wall. Last year was a bad year, and by August we had to make the hard decision as to whether we should go on watering the garden and run the risk of running out of water for the cattle, or keep it for the cattle and let the vegetables die. After long and anxious discussions the villagers themselves decided where their priorities lay. They decided for their cattle and so all the tomatoes had to die, but they had made the right judgement and it was their own and no-one ever complained.

This rain-water, which is conserved in the reservoir made by the dam, comes from a catchment area of only two or three square kilometres. It probably cost no more than £5,000 to build in 1953, and the maintenance cost over twenty years has been the price of one new valve: a small investment for such a good return. It cannot be calculated in terms of the money the people get from the sale of their vegetables, nor in the increase in weight of the cattle which are as healthy at the end of the dry season as they are at its beginning. Its real and lasting value lies in the fact that the people of Chipapa now know that they have a means of earning a cash income over and above their subsistence, and that gives them confidence to hold their heads high as they face inflation and the soaring cost of living.

Last year in August old Winnie, one of the irrigators, came to see me and said she needed a corrugated iron roof for her new house. I was surprised because Winnie is one of the poorest members of our village. Her husband has left her and she has quite a family to look after. The last time I had been to visit her, she had been living in a thatched shelter, not even with walls of poles and mud, just grass.

"I have paid a man to build me a new house," she said, "and now I want to get a good roof to put on it."

I said nothing, but went over to our local builder to borrow his tape measure and followed Winnie to her house. It was not really much of a house; certainly the builder had used neither spirit level nor plumb-line, but at least the bricks were standing one on top of the other and it had two rooms. I measured it up and worked out the cost of a corrugated iron roof which came to over £20. Winnie was watching me as I turned to her and said,

"Sorry, it is going to cost you an awful lot of money and I am sure you can't afford a metal roof this year with all those children to feed. You had better put a thatch on this year and start saving your money in the Credit Union for next year."

"How much did you say?" she asked, "Tell me in pounds because I still can't manage to count in Kwachas."

"Twenty pounds," I said.

She trotted off to her house and from under the bed she pulled an old black trunk. She came back to me with a wad of notes in her hand.

"Where on earth did you get all that money?" I asked.

"From the tomatoes I sold," she said.

Winnie Shachibe, in a matter of less than five months, had fed her children, bought them their school uniforms and washing powder to wash their clothes, soap and candles and the odd packet of sugar. She had herself paid all the costs of production—the seeds and the cost of taking herself and her tomatoes to market twice or three times a week; she had paid the man who built her cockeyed house, and she still had £50 in her hand.

August 1970: Furrow through the hills

One day I decided to go with my friends to visit Shantumbu, an area which lies five miles due north of Chipapa. There was no proper road, really nothing more than an eroded cattle track through the trees. At one point after negotiating a narrow defile through the rocks, we climbed steeply out of a river bed, and there before my eyes was one of the most lovely sights I have ever seen in Zambia. In August the Central Province landscape is dusty and dry. The colours of the bush were russet brown, black and yellow, tawny like a lion's mane. The trees were bare of leaves, the grass fires had exposed the blackened rocks, but what I suddenly saw was a little green valley set in the hills like an emerald dropped by chance from some jewel-box in heaven.

As we drew near, I saw women and children at work in the fields. There were long straight lines of curly lettuces, Chinese cabbage, tomatoes and onions, and here and there big clumps of green banana trees. There must have been four or five acres under cultivation. There was water, but I could not see where it was coming from. There was no sound of diesel engines, no evidence of overhead electric cables bringing power to silently running pumps, no river or stream in the valley bottom, yet there it was, a richly watered oasis in the middle of nowhere, with people growing the precious fruit and vegetables which everyone in Lusaka is crying out for.

We walked down through the gardens to greet the women, and I noticed how expertly the irrigation channels had been laid, how neatly the rows of crops had been arranged, and how free from weeds the whole garden seemed to be. A little runnel of clear water was flowing through the lettuces, and I assumed it must be coming from some hidden spring away up on the hillside, but I was wrong. The truth about the little stream in the bottom of the dry valley is stranger than any Zambian fiction.

On a farm outside Lusaka, where an old Dutchman had developed a little irrigation system in his garden, a semi-literate labourer called Filipo had learned one of the fundamental principles of hydrodynamics, which is simply that if you can keep water running downhill at a gradient just a little steeper than the contour, you can take it anywhere you like. About the year 1965, the Dutchman returned to his native land, and Filipo came to settle in this desolate place with his wife and family, and his brothers and their families. They are members of Watchtower (Jehovah's Witnesses), and they wanted to get away from the UNIP people who had been bullying them. The only way they could find water in the dry season was to climb the steep hillside on the east side of their valley, and scramble down into a deep cleft of the hills where one of the perennial streams that trickle out of the escarpment flows down into the river below.

The joy of simple things like clean water:
The well at Chipapa

Filipo traced the stream to its source, and found that he was looking down on the other side of the hill from his own valley. He then got the crazy idea that if he could divert the stream from its own valley into his valley, he could have running water for his crops. With his brother he started work with hoe and pick-axe and shovel to lead the water where he wanted it to go. Winding in and out amongst the boulders, under the roots of trees, through gravel and stone, they laboriously hacked and shovelled and dug their way. At one point in order to cross a small ravine, they had to make an aqueduct from corrugated iron sheets supported on bush poles. After working for months on end, they brought the waters of the little stream down into their valley, and started to make their garden.

Soon they were producing more vegetables than they could haul to Lusaka on their bicycles. They decided that they needed a small truck, but they knew that even if they could get the money to buy one, it would be of no use to them unless they could drive it up through the Shantumbu escarpment, where there was only a narrow cycle-track. Again they took to their picks and shovels and made a mile-long road out to the top of the valley. There is one quick way of making money in Zambia, and that is by cutting trees and burning clamps of charcoal to sell in the town. This the two brothers did, and before long they had enough money to buy a little truck.

I suppose if Filipo had been a well-educated man, and had known how to write up a project for the technical planning committee of the Land Use Division of the Ministry of Rural Development, he might have applied for a loan from the Government for his vegetable production scheme before he started. I can just imagine the chairman of the committee introducing the subject at the monthly meeting of his experts.

"Gentlemen, we have a request for assistance from a man who wants to grow vegetables in the Shantumbu area. We have made a preliminary investigation of the project from our aerial photographs. You will see if you look at the maps in front of you that it is intended to take water in a furrow from A to B. Quite a bit of blasting will be required. There is no road into the area so we shall have to use a helicopter to fly in the equipment. I have asked our agricultural economist to do a feasibility study of the marketing angle and of course a cost-benefit analysis, but it is obvious we shall have to turn down this request purely on economic grounds because of course the government would never recoup the capital outlay, not in a hundred years."

I know of course that the number of Filipos in Zambia is few and far between. I know that in too many Zambian villages people booze away the day, and spend the night in drunken stupor. I know that we still must have experts from overseas to help us build the dams we need. But somewhere along the line since we achieved our Independence, the link has been severed between the 'expert' with the technical know-how and the common man.

The Zambezi Valley story

In the heyday of the Central African Federation, Roy Welensky proposed building the Kariba Dam on the Zambezi River, creating the largest man-made Lake in the world. This meant removing large numbers of the Valley ba-Tonga from their ancestral homes along the banks of the Zambezi, and settling them amongst the rocky hills on the margins of the Lake. They were given the order to move, but the ba-Tonga did not believe the Zambezi would ever be dammed. When it did happen and the waters began to lap the doorways of their homes, they still refused to move. Jonas Jones, the Secretary of Native Affairs in the Northern Rhodesia government, who had laid on lorries to remove the people, was faced with an agonising decision. Should he let the ba-Tonga drown or should he remove them by force? He took a gamble. Believing that a moderate display of armed troops would sufficiently intimidate the recalcitrant ba-Tonga, he went down into the Valley and read them the riot act.

"The people must move," he said. The ba-Tonga brandished their spears. The soldiers cocked their rifles. A single mu-Tonga threw his spear. The soldiers fired and five ba-Tonga lay dead on the ground. The next day, they, their wives and children, their chickens and their goats, climbed sheepishly onto the removal trucks and were carried away to the 'resettlement' areas.

Traditionally the ba-Tonga had lived a hard but prosperous life in their big villages along the banks of the Zambezi River. In July when the flood waters began to recede, leaving rich deposits of alluvial soil, they had planted their maize and pumpkins. These they called their Zilili gardens, and no other tribe in the whole of Zambia had been given such a wonderful gift. Their cattle too, which survived through the dry season on the young leaves of the mopani trees, found rich grass for grazing. Once they were moved, however, many ba-Tonga died of a broken heart. Some learned to fish in the Lake and others tried to farm, but the mopani soil was too hard to dig with a hoe in the dry season and too 'sticky' to cultivate in the rains; anyway there was little fertility in the land, which was why the mopani trees were growing there.

Ten years after Kariba Lake had filled to the brim, two white Agricultural Officers visiting the area of Chief Mwemba, reported that what little land remained after the flooding of the Lake had been destroyed by the ba-Tonga themselves. There was no solution to their problem but to move them once again to virgin land high up on the plateau. As a member of the Land Resettlement Board, I was asked to go down into the valley and tell them they simply had to move. Chief Mwemba called

Chipapa's key resource: the dam

a big meeting of all the Headmen and in no uncertain terms they said, "No way are we going to move again." The Chief himself knew that if they did move, it would be into another Chief's area, and he would lose all his power. I knew very well, as the agriculturalists did not, that there is no love lost between the Valley ba-Tonga and the Plateau ba-Tonga; they even speak a different dialect. I returned to Lusaka and reported to the authorities that the ba-Tonga would never move. However I believed that there might be a solution if a way could be found to teach them how to irrigate the land.

At this point Dr Krapf saved my bacon. I had come to know him well on his appointment by the World Council of Churches to the Mindolo Ecumenical Foundation to start the first Lay Training Institute in Africa. It was there that he met Kaunda, and must have so impressed him that some months later the President appointed him, with two other Europeans, to be his advisers on social policy. This was my problem: it was not economic or political, it was clearly social. Kaunda had made me a Resettlement Officer and had sent me down into the Zambezi Valley to persuade the Valley Tonga to move, and they had blankly refused. Sending in the troops as the Colonial Government had done ten years previously was not an option, so I turned to Dr Krapf. "Could you help the ba-Tonga and me by finding, through your wide-ranging contacts in Germany, a high-powered irrigation expert?" A few weeks later Dr Garbrecht, a world expert on irrigation who had just returned from advising the government of Turkey, arrived by plane from Berlin.

I flew down with him to meet Chief Mwemba, and on a small airstrip deep in the bush we were met by a Land-Rover. We travelled through large tracts of *mopani* forest, and at one point we got out of the car and, taking a hoe in my hand, I showed him how hard the soils could get in the dry season. I lifted the hoe high above my head and made a swipe. The hoe bounced back in my face. As we travelled together through the forest and along the Lake shore he turned to me and said, "Compared to Turkey, this is a Garden of Eden." By enquiring from local people we discovered that there were at least two places where, during the rains, little rivers flowing into the Lake had left small patches of alluvial soil in their tiny 'deltas'. Garbrecht quickly realised that these might be used for irrigation. Either the streams might be dammed near their source high up on the Plateau to irrigate these small patches of land by gravity; or diesel engines might be installed to pump water from the Lake.

When Garbrecht had written his report I took it to the authorities. They hummed and ha'ed, admitted that the German professor certainly had a point, but was he being practical? They called him to the office and said, "We do appreciate all that you have done. If we had a surplus staff of Agricultural Officers we would consider your plan. However one by one, the Agricultural Officers have left this country. We have no-one to teach the ba-Tonga to be irrigators."

When I heard their decision I went back to Dr Krapf. "It is a funny thing," he said, "but I have recently been in touch with a group of people in Germany called 'the Gossner Mission'. They believe in mission, but not mission by clergy who have been trained only in theology. They believe that the best missionaries are laymen who use their hands to put their faith into daily practice. They have until now been working in India, where they have been so successful that the Indians themselves have set up their own church which they call the 'Gossner Indian Church'. They feel that it is time to move on to other fields."

"What?" I said to Dr Krapf. "God must be joking. Just you get that Gossner leader to come out pronto to meet Kaunda and see for himself the problems we have here in Africa."

The upshot was that I drew up a serious plan outlining exactly what was required. We needed six people: a team leader, three agriculturalists, a builder and a nurse. I would give them all caravans so that they could go down and live with the people in the Zambezi Valley. I would absolutely insist that they learn to speak Ci-Tonga and I would arrange for one of our Methodist missionaries, Reverend Cecil Hopgood, the translator of the Tonga Bible, to go over for six weeks to Germany to give them preliminary instructions. When they arrived they would take their caravans to the Roman Catholic Mission at Chikuni, where for another three months they would receive further instruction.

Using my authority to write 'requisition orders', I purchased six caravans for the team. The leader was married with one small child, so I bought him, from South Africa, a longer and more luxurious model. In addition I arranged for them to have a massive four-wheel-drive five-ton truck painted brilliant white. The Germans called it their 'white elephant' (not of course understanding what we English mean by that enigmatic phrase). In fact it proved invaluable to them, especially during the heavy rains.

They were all delightful and dedicated people, with little idea of what it was really like to live in the isolated and extremely hot Zambezi Valley, but their enthusiasm was unbounded. The 'pioneer' contingent went down first, with instructions to survey suitable sites and start building permanent houses. Kriebel their leader would follow a few days later. He was not in fact a layman, but a minister in the Church in Germany. A quiet unassuming man who at first seemed an unlikely choice as leader, he quickly showed that he had a gift with languages and soon outstripped the others in his knowledge of Ci-Tonga.

Most of the team brought their own Volkswagen Beetles, but the Mission provided Kriebel with a long-wheelbase Land-Rover. He used this to tow his new caravan into the Valley. Setting off alone from Lusaka he crossed the Kafue River and climbed up the Munali pass but when coming down from the top he felt his caravan swaying from side to side. Finally it tipped over, depositing him and his Land-Rover upside down in a deep ditch. Shaken but unhurt he clambered out to see his caravan in a thousand pieces and his Land-Rover's wheels still spinning in the air, the vehicle apparently a total wreck. The superstructure was squashed flat, and how he survived no-one knew. Perhaps being a small man he slid down to the floor.

I expected a rocket from the Permanent Secretary, but nothing happened, so I assumed that the Government in their affluence simply wrote off the debt. Meanwhile the building programme was suffering from long delays. The rains had come and it was insufferably hot in the Valley bottom. Kriebel came to see me and said that I was expecting far too much of the Gossner team, and they would have to withdraw. That was exactly what had happened to the first missionaries fifty years before. They had withdrawn to the Plateau and built themselves houses at Masuku.

Then another funny thing happened. The Minister of Agriculture, my friend from the days of the 'struggle', told me to meet him in the Valley because he had been offered a place built by a European road contractor which he thought might be suitable for the setting up of a new Government agricultural station. The Italian construction firm, which for a period of over two years had built the road from the Plateau down into the Valley, had finished its work and was about to evacuate its staff. They were offering six family houses, built from concrete blocks, with metal trusses for the roofs, doors and windows. There were also workshops, garages, a line of single rooms and best of all, a pumped water supply—all for £50,000.

I talked it over with the Minister and pointed out that this place at the foot of the hills was both isolated from the villages and without suitable agricultural land for miles around. It was hardly the place for an agricultural training centre. He agreed, and said it was mine if I could raise the £50,000. Of course I did not have such a sum, but what a wonderful place to settle the Germans.

I got in touch with the Italian contractors and taking the bull by the horns pointed out that it was a bit of a cheek on their part to ask £50,000 because, when they had first negotiated the deal with the Government, the cost of the buildings had been included in the original contract. They had no title to the land so I would pay them nothing, to which they replied, "If you will not pay we will strip off all the iron sheets, the doors and the window frames and remove the diesel pump and leave you with a ruin."

I had to have this place, otherwise the Germans would leave. My requisition form would hardly bear the cost of £50,000, so I went to see Peter Stutley, the Permanent Secretary of the Ministry, with whom I had struck up a firm friendship.

"Peter," I said, "I am in a jam and I don't know what to do."

"Yes," he said. "You have a flair for giving us problems in the Ministry, but what good is a ruin? I think you should offer the Italians £15,000. I think I know how to pull the right strings. Leave it to me."

The Germans moved in, and two years later I was invited down to the Valley to watch the precious water of the Lake flow onto the beautifully-contoured fields of the irrigation project. Later during a period of severe drought, when the diesel pumps could be moved no nearer the margins of the Lake, I realised that we should have adopted Garbrecht's other alternative and built dams up on the Plateau.

After a time the other teams—Dutch, British and Swedish—all made a significant contribution in the areas to which I had sent them, but in the end they left. The Germans, however, with amazing tenacity of purpose stayed on. All through the years when the Southern Rhodesian white soldiers laid mines on the Lake shore roads, they never gave up. The irrigation was not a spectacular success, but the fact that the Ci-Tonga speaking Germans were able to create lasting relationships with Chief Mwemba and his people gave them new confidence in their future. The 'temporary' accommodation is still in use after thirty-five years; the borehole has never dried up and the houses are occupied by well-trained African staff.

The Chilota Bus

17

I BEGAN MY LIFE IN CHIPAPA hoping that I could rely on my bicycle to commute to town, but I soon changed to using my wife's little ten-year-old Ford Popular. I think the most powerful argument made by the Chipapa people when they discussed whether I should be allowed to live in the village, was simply that any man with a car is an enormous asset to the community.

I was to be the only car owner in the whole area, and the consequences of that I was soon to discover, for the sun never rose but it revealed a little huddle of people with their bundles at my caravan door, needing lifts to the clinic at Chilanga or to town.

The Ford Popular was made in Britain after World War II as the people's utility car, and if anyone needed to be persuaded of the quality of British workmanship at that time, he should have seen us chugging up the hills to Lusaka with two on the bucket seat beside me in the front, and four behind, and the boot flap down, piled high with bundles.

The first lesson I had to learn is that there is no such thing as a 'private' car in a village. It has to be a people's car, but mine was too small for this role, and more were left behind than I could take. Then I had a stroke of luck: I was given the temporary use of a two-ton Dyna Diesel. The village carpenter helped me make wooden seats in the back, and everyone rejoiced because no-one was ever left behind on the road, and everyone who wanted it got a free ride into town in the morning, and a free ride back. That is, everyone rejoiced but me. It is one thing to feel virtuous as the village saviour, but quite another to be at everyone's beck and call in any emergency from hospitalising pregnant women in the middle of the night, to taking mourners to a funeral on Saturday afternoon. There were problems too with the police, who simply could not believe that I was not running a lucrative private bus service, and when I stopped at the South End roundabout in Lusaka to pick up my returning Chipapa passengers, all the other people waiting there wanting lifts to Chilanga and Kafue climbed aboard, and it might take half an hour to persuade them to get off. If they persisted, I just had to carry them and keep stopping all along the road, and the Chipapa passengers would get furious with the delay because the women had promised to get back to cook their husbands' evening meal, and I didn't want to start breaking up the Chipapa marriages.

My problem was temporarily solved when I walked out of the situation and went back to Britain for a few months to front Christian Aid's World Poverty Campaign, but I took Chipapa's problem with me, because the people had been put right back where they were before; as they said, 'crying for transport'.

By 1971 we had begun to work out together in our Ward Development Committee what we thought could be a possible solution to the problem which loomed larger and larger in the minds of the people, as they began to need transport to get their produce to market. Here is a statement of our thinking at that time:

A. *The Need*

The people of Chipapa are in great need of transport for the following reasons:

1. To get children and their mothers and old people to the clinic at Chilanga.
2. To get seriously sick people to hospital in Lusaka in good time.
3. To enable relatives to go to Lusaka to visit sick people or when a person has died.
4. To get vegetables and chickens and eggs to the Lusaka market.
5. To do shopping.
6. To catch the train or bus in Lusaka when making a journey to a far place.
7. To get supplies of more things such as soap, paraffin, sugar, matches and candles for sale in the small local shops.

B. The Problem

1. The Chipapa road is not served by any kind of public transport. The United Bus Company of Zambia cannot agree to run a service until the number of regular passengers increases.

2. The distance is only twenty miles from Chipapa School to Lusaka, but not enough people travel each day to make it economic to make more than one journey to town each day.

3. Some days too many people want to travel and on other days there are very few.

4. Most people who are sick, especially women with sick children, cannot afford to pay money every time they go to the clinic at Chilanga for treatment.

5. If a full-time driver is employed and given a proper monthly wage, he will spend all day in town doing nothing, but he will expect to be paid for sitting and doing nothing.

6. If a small vehicle is used for transporting people and their bundles, it will often leave many people standing by the roadside without help. If a big vehicle is used, it is very expensive to buy and to keep running, and often it will run half empty. A taxi is too small and a bus too big.

C. A Possible Solution

The problem has been discussed with many people including the Road Traffic Commissioner, to discover all about the legal side of running a bus service. The long-term solution would be for one man to set up a transport business and a garage, and run an efficient bus service for the people, or the Bus Company should do it. However it will be some years before it becomes economic for one man to run a service, and the Bus Company cannot run a service on a route with few passengers when there are not even enough buses on the main routes and in the towns.

The people of Chipapa who are able to take vegetables and other things to market can afford to pay some money and also people earning salaries such as teachers, but the whole cost cannot be met by the people.

Transportation to and from Chipapa must be somehow subsidised over the next five or six years.

When the prosperity of the area increases, the people will be able to afford the full cost of a bus service. A bus service can be subsidised in a number of ways. The most important being:

a. No person or group of persons should make a profit out of this service to the people.

b. The richer and more educated members of the Chipapa community should offer help and assistance to those who are poor and sick.

c. Outside people can be asked to give help in buying the first vehicle. The Central Government, or Rural Council, or a charitable agency could be asked to help with the money.

It is now proposed that the Ward Development Committee do the following:

a. Seek in every possible way to find £1,000 for the purchase of a strong pick-up truck (about 1.5 tons).

b. Find one trustworthy person in the community who would take charge of the vehicle, making sure that it is properly serviced and kept in good order.

We had felt the need, we had analysed the problem, and we had made our plan, but the plan did not work. The reasons why it did not work were not first of all financial and technical, they were 'people' problems. We thought that the Ward Development Committee was the proper place to thrash out the issue and that the Ward was the right community to handle it, but we were wrong. Ward Seventeen was created for Local Government electoral purposes. It was created by people who drew lines on maps to enclose a certain number of voters, but those boundaries took no notice of the needs and aspirations of the people who lived within them.

Ward Seventeen is made up of two separate and distinct communities, those of Chipapa and Chipongwe. The Chipapa people live in the seven little villages round the dam, and the centre of their life is the school and irrigated garden. They occupy the land under the customary law of usage, and they are all knit together in an inextricable web of family and kinship relationships. The Chipongwe people on the other hand are immigrants from many different tribes, living on old state land farms owned by absen-

tee landlords. Legally they are squatters. As they live closer to the main
tar road running north to Lusaka and south to Kafue, they have access to
the state bus service, and they can get 'Zamcabs' and private taxis in an
emergency.

When we divided the Ward up into nine sections, and appointed leaders in each section to explain the idea of raising money for a bus by every
family subscribing £1.00, they all agreed, but when the time came to put
the money on the table, the Chipongwe people all said that their exis-
tence as squatters was so precarious that they might be moved before
the bus was bought, and so they would lose their money. The Chipapa
people said that if the Chipongwe people did not subscribe they could
not possibly reach the target; and then a big argument developed about
whether a man with two or more wives should pay more than £1.00.
Some said that a man with two wives was richer because he had more
labour to work his gardens, and so could afford to pay more; others said
that a man with two wives was poorer, because he had more children to
support. They managed very effectively to avoid making a decision about
their problems.

But all this time the problem was growing, and the Chipapa people
were getting desperate to find some way of getting their tomatoes, cabbages, peas, and beans to market. Although I would help whenever I could,
I was often away for weeks at a time.

More and more people were travelling the road, and at this point two
separate ideas began to emerge. The first came from the Chipapa people,
who said that although they could not themselves raise the £1,000 needed,
they might be able to get a loan to buy a second-hand vehicle and get a
driver, and pay off the loan from the money they would get transporting
their vegetables to market.

The other idea came from a man in the area who saw a chance of making some money out of the situation. Our local 'rich man' found out that
he could get a loan for two-thirds of the capital required to buy a mini-bus
from the government, if he put down the other third, and if he could get a
franchise from the Road Service Commissioner for the route in question.
He thought that there would not be enough passengers from the Chipapa
and Chipongwe areas alone to make it pay, so he applied for an extended
route to serve the people right down at Chiaba on the Zambezi on two
days a week, and serve the local people on the other five. He found he

could purchase a sixteen-seater mini-bus for £2,500, so he sold his herd of cattle to get his equity of £800 and bought the bus. He employed as a driver a cheerful young man who said he had a PSV licence, and was an experienced mechanic. He also took on another young man as conductor to collect the fares. Everyone was delighted and the bus was on the road from early morning until late at night. The more it travelled, the more passengers used it and the more money came in, even though sometimes it travelled half-empty.

Meanwhile I was able to help the Chipapa vegetable growers get hold of a second-hand one-ton pick-up with a wooden canopy and a roof rack. If they packed it tightly, they could carry eight passengers sitting on the floor of the vehicle, and up to half a ton of vegetables on the roof. Their main problem now was to find a driver. They had a meeting and said that whoever drove their vehicle must be good with a clean licence, he must be absolutely honest, and he must be known never to touch beer. The trouble was that they thought they would never find such a person, unless he would come down out of heaven. In fact there was one man in the village who had a driving licence, so they took him on, even though they could only offer to pay him 50p a day.

He did marvellously for one week, and then he did not come home one night until very late, and it was found that he had been using the vehicle as his own private taxi when he got to town. So they said, "We had better start at the other end. We will find a man who does not drink and is as honest as any man can be in this wicked world, and we will teach him to drive."

There was a man called Mr Phiri who had married a local woman. He used to work in a Lusaka bakery, but he had moved to Chipapa where he had built a little shop. It was not a very successful enterprise, because he always seemed to run out of stocks of candles and matches and sugar and salt just when people wanted them. We asked Mr Phiri if he would agree to be our driver if we could teach him to drive. He had never held the steering wheel of a car before, but he said he would try, and he started taking lessons in Lusaka. He did not pass the driving test the first time, but he did the second, and he began cautiously to drive the old pick-up to Lusaka every day.

I wanted him to take over from me the emergency trips that I some-times had to make at night, but I never seemed to find the time to take him

Chipapa Vehicle 3: the Chiloto Bus

out at night to show him how to handle the van in the dark. One evening the sun set and Mr Phiri had not arrived home. Someone told me that he had taken the car up the valley the nine miles to the school at Chilambila to collect some teachers who had sent word that they needed him. I was surprised that he had the nerve to drive along that narrow twisting road through the hills, crossing the stony stream beds, and climbing up out of the drifts. Anyway, I thought, he will be sleeping there, and he will drive back in the morning, so I went to bed. I had no sooner put the light out, than I heard the familiar sound of the pick-up's engine, but I was puzzled because there was no light coming in through the window on that side of the house. I went outside and Mr Phiri was just locking the car door. "That must have been quite a drive," I said, "the first time you have ever driven at night."

"Yes," he said, "I couldn't go very fast, that is why I am a bit late. The head and sidelights failed so I had to drive using the flashing indicators."

Mr Phiri looked after the car very well, always checking the oil and washing it down on Sunday morning, but one day the engine developed a knock. We towed it into the garage at Makeni and when they stripped it down, they told us that a most unusual thing had happened: one of the pistons had disintegrated, and the repair would cost over £250.

Our vehicle was off the road for two months but the local rich man was laughing. He fixed a roof rack onto his mini-bus, and carried the vegetables to market, but he didn't laugh for long, because while his young driver was having the time of his life careering back and forth between Chiaba and our village and Lusaka he didn't worry too much about checking the oil, and he always believed that the faster you drive and the more journeys you could make, the more passengers you could carry and the more money you could jingle in your pocket. The mini-bus was not really designed for country roads; it was made for the cities, and within a few months the engine was worn out. However many times the young driver took it to pieces laying the parts carefully on the dusty ground, and putting them back with new bearings or shims or con-rods, it never worked again.

So the rich man lost all his cattle, and all the money he had taken was spent on petrol and overtime to his driver and the bus conductor, and in the end of course he could not pay back his loan, so the finance company had to repossess the bus and sell it for what they could get. No doubt in their annual report they will blame the 'irresponsible borrower' for not paying his debts, but they will write it off and lead some other poor sucker up the garden path, never bothering to take care to find out whether he has the experience to manage a tricky thing like a transport business. But most of the blame should lie with the garage which sold him the mini-bus. All they cared about was to get the vehicle out of their glossy show-room, and get the money from the sale of the cattle, and the loan from the finance company safely into their own pockets, and the pockets of the mini-bus manufacturers in Europe and Japan.

But even when the Chipapa people got their vehicle back on the road again, without competition from the rich man, they were not quite out of the wood. They were doing remarkably well and meeting all the running costs, and they were beginning to pay off their loan, but this meant packing the back of the vanette with the maximum number of people possible. People just had to get to town, even if it meant dropping down the tail board and sitting with their legs dangling a few inches from the ground. Quite rightly the police could not allow this to go on, and they finally impounded the car and took Mr Phiri to see Mr Banda the Road

Traffic Commissioner. He just said flatly, "Never more than three in the back and one passenger with the driver in front."

There were no two ways about it. We just had to get a bigger bus. It was then that I suffered my great temptation. When I came into town in the morning I would see the officials of the Bank of Zambia being driven to work in mini-buses, and the National Brewing Company had built a great big seven-ton forty-seater to transport their staff to the brewery. All these people could have cycled to work if they had to. But the women of Chipapa, even if they wanted to, could not cycle to market with their tomatoes, nor carry sick children to the clinic at Chilanga. I longed to give the poor of Chipapa their own spanking new bus with twice as much chromium plate as the Bank of Zambia bus. I wanted to dress Mr Phiri in a chauffeur's uniform with gold-braided epaulettes and a blue peaked cap and white kid gloves. And I could have done if I had tried. All that was needed was a well-worded, heart-string-tugging letter to Christian Aid or Oxfam; that was my temptation, but I kicked the devil in the crutch and did the right thing. I started working with the members of the little Credit Union in the village, and said that if only they would start saving the money they were making from their vegetables, and if they would really work at it, and pull together and save, they could get the money for

Getting the tomato harvest ready for market, carried by Merfyn's vanette and later by the Chiloto bus

the down payment on a new bus. They are not that poor. Some of them have got cattle and if they really put their minds to it they could do it.

But they didn't. For the peasants of Chipapa, there is no tomorrow for which you can save today. They have learned by bitter experience that the future is dark with impending calamity. If you can manage to store away a little money in a hole in the ground, it must be kept hidden in a secret place, only to be brought out in time of dire need, which means great sickness or the death of someone in the family. They knew that the little pick-up was too small, they knew that sooner or later it would break down or wear out, they knew it was running illegally, but as long as Mr Phiri kept it going they would put off the need to raise money for a new one. I knew we had to have a new vehicle, and I knew it was not any good handing it to the people on a plate, because they had to feel it was their own and that they had worked to get it, so I began to talk with them about what they knew they needed.

They knew that a mini-bus like the rich man's mini-bus was not the answer. It must be bigger but not too big. It must be strong enough to stand the bashing it would get on the Chipapa road, but not as big as the brewery bus. We began to get a picture of what we needed. It should be a three-tonne chassis with a Zambian-made body, built to our requirements. It must have a door at the back, with bench seats for ten people each side, and a seat for two or three across the end with their backs to the cab. There must be windows down both sides, but not opening windows, because those are much too expensive. The two windows up front would simply be left as open spaces to let the air in. The main floor space must be left free, so that people could pile in their boxes of tomatoes and bags of cabbages and beans, and crates of chickens and even a bicycle or two if necessary. With plenty of floor space the bus could be used on Saturdays to take the football teams for matches at the neighbouring schools.

I began making enquires in Lusaka from the garages to see what a three-ton chassis would cost. They said £2,500. I went to the engineering firms to see what it would post to build on a custom-made body. They said £1,000, but with the price of steel going up it might be £1,500 in a few months' time. The situation was utterly hopeless, because even if the people managed to raise £500 and we got a finance company to give us a loan for the rest, they would demand repayment over two years at 12.5%, and we should never be able to pay it off. We would have to find something cheaper. A motor company had recently opened up a new branch in Lusaka Road. I went to enquire about the price of a chassis and explained what we needed. The manager gave me a funny look and said, "I've got something in the back that might interest you, come and see."

I walked into the new big shed at the back. It was like one of those huge empty warehouses you see on a dockside waiting for a shipment of goods. Standing right in the middle of this great commercial cathedral was our dream bus, made exactly to our plan. There it stood, all new, and blue, shining in the morning sun which filtered through the transparent corrugated fanlights in the roof. I asked, "Who did you make it for?"

He said, "It's a bit of a sad story. We made it for one of the mining companies up on the Copperbelt to carry their workers, and sent it up there, but they sent it back. They said it was no use because the windows don't open and there is not enough ventilation for the people travelling inside. Besides, the mine workers union wouldn't pass a home-made thing like that! I'm afraid there is nothing for it, but to take the body off and replace it with a flat-bed body and sell it as an ordinary truck."

"How much do you want for it?" I asked.

"£2,750," he said.

A Parliament of Birds 18

I HAD TO FIND £2,750 and find it quickly, if the Chipapa dream was going to come true. But that sort of money doesn't grow on trees. If only I had a rich friend to give us a temporary loan until we could organise the money! But the rich don't travel our road in Chipapa, so we never meet them there to make them our friends.

Then I remembered that round the corner from the garage where the blue bus stood in all its glory, was Jukes Curtis. We were friends when we had once been poor together, in the early days at Mumbwa. I was then an impecunious missionary, and he was a businessman with too many irons in the fire, and not one of them hot. Well some of his irons in the end did get hot, red hot, so his problem became not how to make money, but how to put his money to good use. I was already in debt to this man, not because he had ever made me a loan, but because he saved me from becoming a one hundred percent socialist.

When I see the 'wicked' white capitalists exploiting the poor down-trodden peasants, then I am sometimes tempted to declare that Zambia's only path to economic sanity must be along the nationalisation road. But when I stop talking about the 'masses' and start talking to Daniel and Sarah and the others, I find that they get a much better deal from that 'wicked' white capitalist who is my friend, than from the giant para-statal transport organisation that competes with him in the same way of business. The other thing is that while he has grown rich by running an efficient and well jacked-up family business, it has cost the government millions of pounds to run their undisciplined, extravagant, and over-staffed para-statals. So although capitalism has its ugly face in Zambia, it is really no uglier than the state's monsters whose towering concrete castles disfigure the human face of Cairo Road in Lusaka.

So I went round the corner to see Jukes, and there he was—not in a carpeted and air conditioned room on the fifteenth floor of the latest Lusaka skyscraper, but in his dusty office at 'the yard' surrounded by his yellow painted trucks and trailers and tankers. I had to pass through no protective screen of busily chatting typists, I walked straight through the open door of his office and said, "Jukes, I have found me a truck and I want you to buy it for me."

"What do you mean you want me to buy you a truck?"

"Well, it's not really for me; it's for the Chipapa people, and I don't really want you to buy it, I just want you to lend us the money."

"Bit of a risk isn't it, to put a truck in the hands of a bunch of villagers who can hardly look after their own bicycles, and have never driven anything faster than an ox cart? Anyway, how much do you want, and how are you going to pay me back? I've always said I'm prepared to help anyone who can show me he is helping himself, And where is it? I'm not going to let you buy a pig in a poke. Let's go and see it."

So we went round to see it in the big empty warehouse. It was standing over an open inspection pit, so he got down underneath and had a good look at the suspension.

"How much is he asking for it?"

"Only £2,750 and a new one would cost £4,000 and ..."

"Too much," he said. "I'll knock him down by £250."

"But supposing someone else comes in and offers him a bit more?"

"Don't be daft, man. He wouldn't be asking £2,750 if it's worth not a penny more than £2,500. What I have got to decide is whether I can take the risk of knocking him down by four hundred, not two fifty."

I kept my fingers crossed while he was making up his mind. Jukes made the deal, which I thought was a very fair one (and one that other rich men might do worse than to follow): he said that for every pound invested by the people of Chipapa in their bus, he would invest another pound. Remember, the people at that point had raised nothing.

Now I was faced with the $64,000 question. What would the people of Chipapa do? I went to Chipapa and on the Saturday morning I brought the Headmen and some of the elders to see the shining bus. At first they couldn't believe their eyes and said it must be a gift from heaven. "No way," I said, "it belongs to the man in the garage, and he will only sell it to us if we in Chipapa make a really serious effort to get the money to put down a substantial deposit." They said they would go back to Chipapa and discuss it with the people and let me know. I gave them two weeks and said we would meet on Sunday 30 June at 0900 hours, and there must be no promissory notes. All that the man at the garage was interested in was hard cash.

On Saturday 29 June, Sarah killed the last of our flock of Emden geese. It was a big bird and too large to go into my little oven, so Sarah stewed it for six hours, which was just as well, as the flesh was tough as old boots. But it made the most beautiful soup I have ever tasted, and was more than enough for all the visitors who came that weekend.

Early next morning, Sarah knocked on my door and said, "A stranger has come."

"Where is he?" I asked.

"In the chicken run."

"What do you mean, 'In the chicken run'?"

"It is a very big bird."

"Did it fly in?" I said.

"No, it just came walking down the path and stood outside the gate asking to be let inside the wire to feed with the hens and the Muscovy ducks."

I walked over to the hen run and there she was: a wild spur-winged goose. Her black and purple wings glistened in the morning sun and she held her head high on her proud and splendid neck; a wild goose which looked at us with steady eye and seemed strangely to show no trace of fear. Daniel, rubbing the sleep from his eyes, came out of his house to see the stranger and I caught him looking round for a stick to clobber her. He didn't see a wild goose there; he saw some meat for the pot. I didn't blame him, because once I had killed a wild hare that got trapped in the house. I killed it with my bare hands because I too had been in need of meat. But as we watched the wild goose eyeing us and curving down her neck to feed, we knew that we were not to kill her.

When the time came for the meeting, I went to the courthouse, but no one came. It had been a cold night with hoar frost in white patches on the ground, so people were in no hurry to crawl out of their blankets or leave the sweet potatoes roasting in the warm embers of the previous night's fire. By ten o'clock they came straggling in, some with ten pounds and some with five and some with only one 50p coin in their hands. At 10.30 hours Yoram, the retired cook who owns the grinding mill, came forward out of the little crowd and laid a bundle of notes on the table. We counted them and there were 10 ten pound notes, one hundred pounds. Everyone clapped and there was a buzz of conversation. Then Elisa brought twenty which she had saved from the sale of vegetables last year. Daniel went to get his Bible and started preaching about the talents. He was reading the words of the Master, "Well done thou good and faithful servant ...", when Mr Phiri walked in. We all knew that none of us would ever have given a penny for the bus unless we had confidence in our servant the driver, and he showed the confidence he had in himself and in them by laying his hundred pounds on the open pages of the Bible.

Everyone was very happy, because now we could go in the morning to collect the bus which had been waiting in the garage. That is what we did, but still a little doubt was niggling at the back of my mind. We had done the sums over and over again, and in four years we could pay off the loan with interest if everything went smoothly. But I had heard that week that the cost of petrol had doubled, and for a three-ton truck with a petrol engine, the cost of fuel is the major running cost. It looked as if the whole venture might come unstuck for a reason beyond our control. If the vehicle cost so much to run that there would be no 'profit' each week to pay back the loan, then the promises we had made to the investors, that is the people of Chipapa and Jukes and Iain McDonald of 'War on Want', would all be empty. Then the people would blame the driver and Jukes would say, "I told you so," and Iain would never trust one of those "bloody Englishmen" again. And all because the Arabs, like a brood of pythons, were squeezing us to economic death. Let them squeeze the Americans and the British and the Japanese and the Germans, they deserve it, but haven't they been squeezing the Developing Countries for long enough? Let them squeeze the West, but surely it isn't fair to squeeze the poverty-stricken peasants of Chipapa.

The next morning, 1 July, I went for a walk by the dam. The patches of white hoar frost were melting in the warmth of a sun, whose slanting rays gave every tree a halo and turned the feathery pampas tops of all the lakeside reeds to a canopy of snow. Suddenly I was made aware of a great celebration such as I have never seen or heard before, and it was going on

The flocks of ducks and geese did a wonderful job of keeping the Chipapa dam free of bilharzia-carrying snails

all around me. Overhead a pair of bateleur eagles were gliding high on motionless wings; then from the west, from behind Chipapa's hill, came beating in a single cormorant, only a little lower in the heavens than the eagles. When he reached the point directly above his mate, who always dries her wings perched on the branch of a fallen tree amongst the reeds, he started a tight spiral and circled down to within a foot of the water's surface and levelled out and skimmed the whole circumference of the lake. I heard a lourie calling from the top of one of the mimosa trees and turned to see only his head with the grey crest rising and falling, silhouetted against the sun. There seemed to be a bird on the highest branch of every tree. A dove alighted on a high twig right next to a grey sparrow-hawk, and a pair of barbets flew from tree to tree beating out their boundaries with their see-saw call of warning. The blue jays had stopped their monotonous scolding of the black and white crows and, climbing vertically into the sky above their tree, came swooping down, the sunlight shining brilliantly through azure wings.

The birds of Chipapa do not sing as sweetly as the birds of England, but they have no need, for their music is in their colour and their flight. Even so, on that morning in July the air was full of the sound of birds.

The liquid notes of the bulbuls were everywhere and the soft call of the pigeons came from the fig trees. The high cry of the eagles and the sound of the plovers answering one another across the water enraptured me and made me stand to listen as to some ancient hymn. What I then saw I have never seen before or since. It was one of those great gatherings of birds around the lake, the accounts of which are still preserved in the folklore of Zambia. It was not the number of the birds, though there were more than I have ever seen before—it was their variety. It was like a parliament with every species sending its own representatives. A sandpiper flew up from under my feet and from the reeds came first the lily-trotters, white breasts and chestnut wings, trailing their long thin legs behind them as they flew, and then a moorhen, which flew so low it left a trail across the ripples of the lake. The pied kingfishers hovered above the surface of the lake on wings that beat so fast you couldn't see their movement, then suddenly they would plummet, dropping like a stone, and rise, each one with a silver fish in its jet-black beak. Amongst the reeds I saw the brilliant flash of a malachite kingfisher, which came to rest on its fishing perch, a reed bent horizontal just above the water. I watched this tiny creature and marvelled that God had bothered to make something so small to be so beautiful.

On the muddy shore were the plovers, which look so undistinguished yet so dapper when they walk by the water's edge, like mindless civil servants on the steps of the Ministry of Rural Development. But when they take off in flight, they are transformed into a kaleidoscope of beating wings, all orange and black and white and grey. Our great white egret who fishes from a mud-bank was joined by a big grey heron, and they seemed to be carrying on a very long and serious discussion about something. I have never seen them stand so close together like that before, and as I watched them there came a glorious bird on lazy wings, a great brown heron whose plumes shone like coppered gold. He came that day and walked majestically along the shore looking for frogs and other things to eat, but I have not seen him again and I'm afraid the school boys have frightened him away with their catapults.

Our lake is not a natural stretch of water: it was made by men with pick and shovel and wheelbarrows and ox-drawn scoops twenty years ago. Man, ever since he was born, has been interfering with nature and disturbing his environment, which is as it should be, as long as he does his interfering gently and with sensitivity. Twenty years ago there were no cormorants, no herons, no kingfishers, no lily trotters, no wattled plovers, no sandpipers and no moorhens or coots. Now they are there, and they have come as the wild goose came to bless this place.

On that morning by our little lake I came to understand the meaning of that great celebration, but at first I did not know what the birds were trying to tell me. It was not until I got to town on Wednesday that I knew. I saw the buses jam-packed full of people going to work and I saw the great crowds of children assembling outside the Barracks' school. They are growing up without the knowledge of the name of a single bird, except perhaps the drongos in the trees and the sparrows which eat the breadcrumbs round the tricycles of the 'stop-me-and-buy-one' Coca-Cola sellers.

We have separated our children from the creation; we have made it almost impossible for them to be meek, so how shall they inherit the earth? We make them into hooligans who turn to violence to snatch their own reward. How I should love to be able to take one of those children from the town school and put a pair of binoculars in her hand, and show her a malachite kingfisher with red beak poised quite still on his bent reed above the water. Why should that privilege be preserved for the children of the rich American tourists who come to visit our game parks, to click their cameras hoping to carry our peace back with them to their restless homes? And then I thought, "Why just one child? Why shouldn't they all come to Chipapa?"

Instead of Mr Phiri sitting all morning in town waiting for his passengers to get their shopping done, and grow fat sipping endless bottles of Coca-Cola, why shouldn't he fill the bus with kids, and take them for a morning's excursion to the village? After all, isn't this what it is really all about? How we can find a way of bridging the widening gap between town and country, rich and poor, the meek and the violent? Up to that Wednesday morning, I had always thought of our dream bus as being a link between Chipapa and the town, but now I understood what the birds were saying: "Use your bus to bring the children of the town to see us here, and let them feel the gold dust of their inheritance run through their fingers. Let them drink the milk and taste the honey."

Time to Leave

Power to the people

In October 1972 I went to Mbeza to witness the final ceremony concluding the traditional mourning for the late Ila Chief Nalubamba, and the initiation of the new Chief Bright Nalubamba in his place.

This was a unique opportunity for me to witness one of the bravest attempts being made in Zambia to graft the most modern concepts of rural development into the traditional structure of African life. The ba-Ila are no ordinary people, and Chief Nalubamba was no ordinary hereditary ruler. He held at the time the position of General Manager of Zambia's largest Credit Union, with a membership of 8,000 and total shares of over half a million kwacha. He is entirely committed to the belief that the Co-operative Movement can become one of the most effective tools for the economic development of the rural areas of Zambia.

All the ba-Ila chiefs were there: Mukobela, Shezongo, Kaingu and Muwezwa from across the Kafue river. We sat under a grass awning outside the old chief's house, and the crowds began to gather, making a circle, in the centre of which the chief mourners shuttled back and forth, sometimes shouting, sometimes crooning their praise songs for the departed. Bare-breasted women with white clay smeared on their faces reminded the spectators of the Chief's past glories and all his wealth of children. The men performed dances which described his cattle, using crooked arms and up-turned hands to show the length and shape of his oxen's horns. One diminutive and wizened old man, with furious face and staring eyes, brandished his hunting spears so viciously that those on the edge of the crowd drew back in fear, lest he might forget they were flesh and blood, not the ghosts of the dead chief's enemies.

The day grew hotter, the crowd increased, the air filled with dust churned by dancing feet. The rich smell of cattle dung and cooking meat, mixing with the sweet stench of *insaku* (beer-mash) tailings, made us feel we were moving back in time to another world more real to us than the line of police Land-Rovers and the plastic crates of bottled beer and sickly Coke. The beating of drums and the noise of happy people talking filled our ears.

At midday the dancers from the Namwala Secondary School arrived. Their coming had been awaited with some excitement, because they are recognised as the best dancers in the whole of Southern Province. We were not disappointed. They put on a display of traditional dancing such as I have never seen equalled during all my time in Zambia. Their vigour, their rhythm, their muscular control, their sheer ability to enjoy themselves, shone through them and captivated the crowd, who ceased to be spectators and became participants. Their play-acting, especially their imitation of their elders, crippled us with laughter, and their exposé of witchdoctors as clever confidence tricksters must have shaken the faith of the most ardent devotees of the magical arts.

Suddenly as I watched this generation of young Zambians expressing themselves totally through a rediscovery of their old culture, I realised that the whole astonishing effort of building Secondary Schools in remote rural areas is being amply justified. Not because it is going to produce the professional men and women and the technicians of the future, but because, almost by accident, young people in an age group that is reaching physical maturity have had a chance to discover for themselves what being a Zambian is really all about.

My last letter to President Kaunda

"When I wrote to you on 1 August, giving you the three reasons why I felt the time had come for me to leave Zambia, you replied:

> Your second point does not impress me. You know my views about the need to internationalise the church and not nationalise it. I only agree with the church being self-reliant in terms of funds, but certainly not personnel. If the church is going to be a uniting force and not a divisive one, we must work ourselves out of this missionary phobia.

It is not consistent with the Christian message, at least not as far as I understand it.

"It is not usual for us to disagree so fundamentally about such a vital issue, so I am going to take the utmost care to explain my point of view. I do this not just because I want you to understand, but because I believe this to be a matter requiring very clear thinking and very great loving, both by the church in Britain, which sent me here as a missionary, and by the church in Zambia, which for thirty years has welcomed me and does not want to let me go.

"By sheer chance, when I was packing my box last week and was going through my old papers, I came across a memorandum that had been tucked between the pages of a Bible. It was written out by hand on paper that has turned yellow over the fifty years since it was penned. It is notes for a missionary address to be given at the Albert Hall in London, to a gathering of about 5,000 Wesleyan Methodists, by Douglas Gray, my father-in-law and the pioneer of Chipembi in Northern Rhodesia, when he was on furlough in Britain in 1922. Having described the great work of building up the Kingdom in remote and virgin territory, he ends by saying:

> One of the most fascinating joys of parenthood is to watch the gradual unfolding of the child's mind and the dawning consciousness of new ideas. In some such way does the fascination grip one's mind in watching the birth of the church in a new country and the gradual unfolding of the new life, the response to the various stimuli given and the almost imperceptible transformation that takes place as the various stages of growth are reached. The time has come when the fruits of our labours are beginning to be seen in the lives of the people.

"Let us have no illusions about how God sent the good news of His Son to us in Zambia. The Gospel could come in no other way than carried by messengers who willy-nilly were part and parcel of the scramble for Africa. When the Rev. Gray spoke to great audiences of missionary enthusiasts in the Royal Albert Hall in Kensington, he knew that the language they would understand was the language of his day. He saw himself as a Joshua sent across the Jordan to spy out the land. The Wesleyan Methodist Church was for him the New Israel and he was one of God's chosen

People. One cannot but stand in awe at his utter dedication to what he always called 'the work' and his diligence and intelligence in doing it. Nor has anyone in our generation ever matched him in sheer devotion and yearning love.

"I am now fifty-four, four years older than you. I have been a missionary for thirty-one years and I am telling you that the time has come for the missionaries to leave Zambia. I find it very difficult to express in cold print what in the agony of my heart I have come to believe. As you said in your letter to me, what I am saying seems to be inconsistent with the Christian message. All I can do is to quote from the letter which I wrote to Jackson Mwape, the president of our Church, when I tried to explain the reasons for my decision to stop being the kind of missionary he wants me to be, and become one of a new breed of missionary now being developed to meet the challenges of the modern world.

Letter to Jackson Mwape, President of the United Church of Zambia

"We know that we can never settle down, that we are on a journey to an eternal city, so we cannot ever live in our past. We do not have to reject the past; we have to interpret in our own way, in our own generation, what we now believe to be the mission of God in the whole world.

"I have come to share the view of many others, that we have now reached the stage in world mission when priority must be given to the local church to become God's instrument of mission. It is this belief beyond all others that prompts me to pull up my tent pegs in the hope that I can be used for the purposes of mission. It is my concern that Zambians and expatriate ministers should find a way together of stating in quite unequivocal terms that the Holy Spirit can be trusted and that the local church is ready for mission. That statement is made most effectively at this time and in this place in Africa by the withdrawal of the Western Missionary from service in the United Church of Zambia. As a minister of this church I have become convinced that the most effective way of freeing the churches for mission is for them to be saved from their dependence on foreign personnel and foreign funds.

"You may well be asking why I have left it so late to speak. Why did I not say what I'm saying now in 1954, or in 1964 when Zambia achieved its political independence? I can only plead that the full measure of the United Church's dependency did not become clear to me until comparatively recently. Perhaps I always kept in my mind the possibility that some way less drastic than the withdrawal of all missionaries and financial aid might still be found. Perhaps I could not face the possibility that I might have to leave a country which I had felt so certainly called to serve and which I had come to love.

"I doubt if it ever occurs to Daniel to stop and ask himself the question why Godfrey and Shachifwa no longer come to church to hear him preach his Missionary Gospel and sing his missionary hymns. I often ask myself that question and this is the answer I get. There is not any Good News for Shachifwa in being told that if he wants salvation he has to give up the polygamous marriage to this third wife. For him it isn't even bad news, it isn't any news at all, it's just nonsense. Why should he waste a Sunday morning listening to a young man's nonsense when he could be having an exciting game of *chisolo* (draughts) with the other old men in the village?

"What is the Good News which Godfrey would hear if he went to church? 'Don't drink, don't gamble, don't commit adultery, learn the Lord's Prayer, the Apostle's Creed, the catechism and repent and be baptized'. Of course that is true, but the Lord Jesus is pleading to be allowed to love Godfrey into His Kingdom, but that would mean finding a job of work for him to do so that he could earn some pocket money for the dance and the beer party on Saturday night. Good news for Shachifwa would be that one of his sons working somewhere along the Line of Rail had decided to come home to look after his old dad during his declining years.

My point is this. The presence of the white missionary from the West at this moment in time obscures the truth of the Gospel. For he comes here expecting to preach a gospel of liberation, but finds himself employed in shoring up the crumbling walls of a prison."

THE FIGHTING PARSON BOWS OUT

REVEREND Merfyn Temple is leaving Zambia at the end of this month after 30 years. Thirty years is a long time by any standards for anyone to live in a foreign country.

It is difficult to tell how much the people of Zambia responded to his kind of love for them. But one thing is certain. The villagers of Chipapa regard Rev. Temple as their saviour and it is easy to understand this if one visits the village, about 30 km south east of Lusaka.

Inspite of the clear directions on how to get to Rev. Temple's hut, it took a good ten minutes to find it. It was hard to find because the hut in which he lives is just like any other hut in the

● Rev Temple (left) and the people he's leaving behind

It's goodbye to 'a part of Zambia'

Incidentally, the only prizes Merfyn Temple ever

It was in 1953 that Merfyn Temple had his first en-

himself in UNIP. It was a trying moment for him to

In 1964, Dr Kaunda invited Rev. Temple to be the deputy director of the newly formed youth organisation, later to be known as the Zambia Youth Service. He left the Youth service in 1965 and was appointed as a personal advisor to the President on the land settlement. Frank Chitambala, now member of the Central Committee, was appointed chairman of the land settlement board and Merfyn Temple became its secretary.

"Although Dr Kaunda had set out clearly the guidelines for regrouping the villages, his concepts became skewed by the planners," says Rev. Temple. "The board was given no statutory powers and it became a paper dragon gnashing its teeth in frustration and breathing out smoke but no fire."

According to him he realised that very little would be achieved by circulating minutes and memoranda round the corridors of Mulungushi House where he was officed.

In 1966 he left his well furnished office at Mulungushi House for Chipapa. There he set up what he calls "experimental Humanism laboratory" for testing the various theories of rural development.

This is the practical side

THE FIGHTING PARSON BOWS OUT
from the Lusaka Times, September 1974

In spite of the clear directions on how to get to Rev. Temple's hut, it took a good ten minutes to find it. It was hard to find because the hut in which he lives is just like any other hut in the village.

The village itself was deserted. A few people were at the first aid post where they received their weekly medical attention. The rest were busy in the gardens behind the hill.

The scene behind the hill looked like a large oasis in the desert. The huge green area is neatly divided into many portions for each farmer.

In the fields, the farmers, numbering about 20, had gathered to discuss how much was to be donated towards the cost of another self-help project.

With the help of Rev. Temple and the Chipapa village development committee, the people there do everything on a self-help basis.

The Chipapa village farmers were not happy: "We are going to suffer
without Rev. Temple here." They gave a number of reasons as to why they
felt that way. They are able to earn a living through growing vegetables as a
result of Rev. Temple's tireless efforts.

Chipapa has good road communication with Chilanga as a result of his
hunger strike and hard talking to the Lusaka rural council to improve the
road. The farmers almost spoke in chorus about Rev. Temple's greatest help
to the villagers: two vans he had put at the service of the people to transport their produce to the markets in Chilanga and Lusaka.

The people of Chipapa regard him very highly. He has been called the
fighting parson, an impractical dreamer, an extremist and an out-of-the-
ordinary person. Some people have known him as a man who calls a spade
a spade.

This is the practical side of Rev. Temple. As a missionary, he has never
wilted in his loyalty to the church in Zambia. Every Sunday he conducts sermons either in Chilanga, Lilayi or in his own little village chapel in Chipapa.

It is remarkable that Rev. Temple has been allowed to remain a minister
of the United Church of Zambia because the record shows that he has
been a thorn in its side. In November last year, he denounced missionaries in
Zambia as being a "third rate replica of the tired old churches in the west."
He said the United Church of Zambia bore little resemblance to the church
he read about in the New Testament.

These remarks will obviously not please the other missionaries and
churchmen who have opposed views on the role of missionaries in Zambia.
But such are the views of the man who is against the "poor peasants of
Chipapa putting their hard-won ngwee into the collection plate on Sunday
mornings so that once in a while an ecclesiastical plutocrat should come
swinging down to them in his motor car, offering them advice on how to
save their souls, but none on how to save their sickly children."

As a member of the Zambian community at large, he has made a number of enemies as a result of equally frank pronouncements. Recently he
raised a storm when he supported a topic that Zambia was a talking nation.
On a TV discussion, Rev. Temple said that Zambians talk and don't do. He
spoke of beer drinking, road safety and church resolutions and annual semi-
nars where much is resolved and little, if anything enforced.

In addition to this, Rev. Merfyn Temple suggested that to lessen road car-
nage, the President should decree that no bars should be built along the high-
ways. He got a few public canings for this remark. Some people felt such a
step was 'impracticable' and others just called it 'day-dreaming' on his part.

When Rev. Temple finally leaves, both his friends and enemies will feel
the vacuum he will leave behind. For the villagers of Chipapa they will miss
his honest dedication to the improvement of their well-being. For them it
is hard to understand that person of his kind could be allowed to leave the
country he sacrificed his life so much for. In his words, the only people who
will be happy to see him leave are the 'pompous bureaucrats.' He was a
thorn in their flesh.

The farewell party

A few months before I left Zambia for good, I went back to Mbeza for
my farewell party. There were twenty-five of us in Chipapa's Chiloto
bus, of whom six were traditional Headmen. We met this time under the
fig tree outside the new council chamber. It still was not quite finished,
but the architect was there with a hammer in his belt and a mouthful of
nails, putting up the ceiling in the spacious room where the Chief would
meet his people, the headmen of his forty villages and other leaders in the
community.

On this occasion the Chief had no need to invite the dance troupe
from the Secondary School. He has divided his area into ten sections, and
each section sends its best dancers to the Mbeza Cultural and Dancing
Troupe. There must have been three or four hundred of us there on that
hot Sunday afternoon, all gathered in the shade of the great fig tree. No
beer had been brewed, and no oxen killed, but everyone had put on their
gayest clothes and we had a party as good as any party on the State House
lawn in Lusaka. There were only two drummers, but how they made their
drums talk! There was one story teller who told us the funniest shaggy-
dog story I have ever heard—all to the accompaniment of the drum and
mimicry of yapping dogs and baying dogs and snarling dogs and growl-
ing dogs. The dancers were neither very old nor very young, except for
one six-month-old baby on her mother's back whose head jiggled up and
down throughout the dance, and who clapped in gleeful delight whenever her mother held her hands above her head. There was a large puppet
doll manipulated by a prone woman swathed in coloured cloth. She was

supposed to be anonymous, but she giggled so much all the crowd had discovered her identity almost before the show began.

The highlight was when the chief dancer came forward, dressed in coloured beads and skins of serval cats. He had a black briefcase in one hand, and in the other a skirt festooned with hundreds of the rattling tops of Coke and Fanta bottles. He laid them on the table in front of us, and out of his briefcase he took a complete telephone, black stand and receiver, with a wire which he ran down under the table. There was no buzzer, so one of the dancing girls came forward with a cowbell. The bead-bedecked dancer dialled a number and the bell rang,

"Give me international exchange please," he said, and the man who was sitting on the ground under the table at the other end of the line replied:

"What number do you want?"

"The manager of the National Bank of Switzerland."

"And where are you calling from, and what is your number?"

"Mbeza 253—you ought to know my number by now."

All this time the drums were beating softly and the rhythm of the dance went on. There was much tapping of the button on the receiver stand and much tinkling of the bell and crackle from the man under the table.

"Hello, hello, hello. Is that the Bank of Switzerland? I want to speak to the manager please. Hello, hello, hello."

"Just hold on a minute, I'm trying to put you through ... the manager is on the line."

"Good morning sir ... very well thank you and hoping you ... everything is very fine up here in Mbeza. I just thought I would give you a ring and tell you that developments are going on very well here. Mbeza is at a high consciousness of development ... thank you very much sir, I must ring off now, so many people are queuing up to deposit their money ..."

The bell tinkled and the drummers stepped up the tempo of their beat. People in the crowd ran into the centre of the circle to join the song and dance, the clapping and the stamping of their feet became a symphony of rhythm, a music of delight. The chief dancer still sitting at the table had put down the phone, and was giving his entire attention to his typewriter. The dancing skirt made up of threaded reeds and bottle tops, under his expert fingers gave out a sound for all the world like any ancient Underwood or Adler. All to the rhythm of the drums, he rang the bell, and moved the carriage back, and whipped invisible sheets of paper from imaginary rollers.

This whole performance was put on for my benefit, because for some years I had been National Chairman of the Board of Directors of CUSA, the Credit Union Savings Association of Zambia. This movement grew rapidly after Independence, and Chief Nalubamba, one of our most enthusiastic board members, wanted me to see how successfully it had taken root in the villages of his chieftaincy. I stood up and congratulated the chief and his people on the amazing progress of Mbeza People's Bank, and then I got a great surprise.

I had let it be known amongst my friends that when I returned to England I would ask the Methodist Church for their continuing support for the new nation of Zambia: in particular for the ba-Ila because the church's first missionaries who crossed the Zambezi in 1889 called themselves "Ba-Ila Ba-Tonga Mission of the Primitive Methodist Church." However, I said half-jokingly, the educational standard of the English is so high that no-one takes any notice of what you say unless you can call yourself a professor or a doctor. I coveted the title of doctor, but Dr Kaunda who was Chancellor of the University of Zambia never took the hint, even though he himself had an honorary doctorate. I need not have worried, because Chief Nalubamba had heard the whisper.

As the clatter of the typewriter fell silent, three men stepped forward from the band of dancers. The first carried an imitation ceremonial lion spear; if it had been for real it would have been smeared with lions' blood. The second carried a calabash decorated with coloured beads for casting bones. The third held a white sacrificial cock with tied legs and flapping wings. The Chief moved forward and said, "Merfyn Temple, with these insignia of office I confer upon you the honorary doctorate of my ba-Ila tribes. After your name you may add the letters D.Ex: Doctor of Experience."

Epilogue:
Return to the First World

Although the Chiloto bus ran very successfully for some years, Mr Phiri found the responsibility of being both driver/mechanic and collector of fares all too much for him. He resigned, and the new driver was not such an honest man. Rampant inflation drove up the cost of repairs and maintenance, and finally the dream faded away, and the bus ended up in a Lusaka scrap heap. Jukes Curtis never did get his money back.

I left Africa in 1974 and came to live in England, where I suffered severe culture shock for two years, before settling down to become the minister of All Saints Methodist Church in Abingdon, near Oxford. In 1982 I retired, and became a grower of organic fruit and vegetables on one and a half acres of borrowed land in the village of Upper Basildon, near Reading in Berkshire.

My life in Africa had become a half-forgotten dream, until one day out of my past came a grey-haired Zambian friend named Job Mayanda, at that time working at the Zambia High Commission in London but still in close contact with conditions in Zambia. He invited me to visit Africa again to help in finding an alternative to farming with hybrid maize seed and chemical fertilizers. So in 1989 I set out to travel with a bicycle from Nairobi to Kariba to see if my newly discovered enthusiasm for ecological agriculture might be of any help. The story of that journey was published under the title *New Hope For Africa*. All these stories, and some others worth re-telling, will make up Volume Two of my memoirs, which we plan to publish later in 2010.

All proceeds from this book go to support the registered charity, Zambia Orphans of AIDS UK (ZOA–UK). Zambia is one of the African countries hardest hit by HIV/AIDS. About 19 percent of children under 18—over 1 million children—are orphans, most of them due to the HIV/AIDS epidemic. Many households are now headed by children, who are forced to forgo the education they need to prepare for a harsh economic environment, as they struggle to care for their younger siblings.

In response to this crisis, ZOA was formed in 2000 by three concerned Zambians, all former Chipembi students, and now has members from across the world. ZOA works through income-generating activities, skills training, and direct provisioning of food, school and medical needs of the children. In all, about 8000 orphans have been reached and assisted through ZOA's efforts, as of September 2009.

ZOA–UK was launched in June 2007 and is raising funds for disbursement to projects in Zambia, which have been appraised and are managed by our Zambian Board of Trustees.

For more information, or to make a donation to ZOA from the UK, please go to www.zambiaorphans.org/zoauk , or contact the treasurer, Jim Potter, at zoauk@hotmail.co.uk.

Lightning Source UK Ltd.
Milton Keynes UK
04 March 2010

150918UK00001B/55/P